How to Understand Church and Ministry in the United States

The Crossroad Adult Christian Formation Program

The Crossroad
Scripture
Study Program
How to Read the Old Testament
How to Read the New Testament

The Crossroad
Theology and Church
History Study Program
How to Read Church History: Vol. 1
How to Read Church History: Vol. 2
How to Understand the Creed
How to Understand Church and Ministry
in the United States

The Crossroad
Christian Living
Study Program
How to Understand Liturgy
How to Understand the Sacraments
How to Understand Marriage
How to Understand Morality and Ethics

Crossroad
Special Interest
Courses
How to Understand Islam
How to Read the World
How to Understand God
How to Read the Church Fathers
How to Read the Apocalypse

Some "How To..." texts, and accompanying study guides,
may be in preparation. For complete up-to-date
information, please write: The Crossroad Publishing Company
370 Lexington Avenue, New York, New York 10017.

Regina Coll

How to Understand Church and Ministry In the United States

A Crossroad Herder Book
The Crossroad Publishing Company
New York

1996
The Crossroad Publishing Company
370 Lexington Avenue, New York, NY 10017

Copyright © 1996 by Regina Coll

Design and typesetting by Rachel Tall

Printed in the United States of America

Library of Congress Cataloging-in-Publication Data

Coll, Regina.
     How to Understand Church and Ministry in the United States /
Regina Coll.
          p.   cm. — (The Crossroad Adult Christian Formation Program)
     Includes bibliographical references.
     ISBN 0-8245-1468-8
     1. Catholic Church — United States — History. 2. Catholic Church — United States — History — 20th
     Century. I. Title. II. Series.
     BX1406 . 2 . C62   1995
     282' . 73—dc20

                                                                                        95-7280
                                                                                        CIP

Contents

1   Who Is Catholic?   1

2   Discovering Our Catholic Roots   14

3   The Church in the United States
     Contributes to the Universal Church   30

4   The Challenge of Vatican II   44

5   Ministry in All Its Diversity   57

6   Redefining the Community   73

7   The Church in America and the
     Universal Church   86

8   Issues Facing the Church of the Future   102

1

Who Is Catholic?

It has been said that Catholics never leave the church. Even those who claim no longer to belong to the Catholic Church usually identify themselves by their relationship with it. We speak of lapsed Catholics and fallen-away Catholics. We hear, "I am an ex-Catholic," "I was brought up Catholic," or "I am a former Catholic." We don't hear about ex-Lutherans, or lapsed Methodists, or fallen away Baptists.

It seems that there is something about being Catholic that has nothing to do with being registered in a parish, adhering to rules and regulations, or obeying the hierarchy. There is a "Catholic imagination," a Catholic sense of being and of seeing the world that we may find hard to articulate but that is hard to lay aside. Perhaps in some sense it is true that "once a Catholic, always a Catholic."

The word *Catholic* as defined by the dictionary means "broad and general scope; universal, all-inclusive; broad and comprehensive in interests, sympathies, or the like, liberal."

When some critics maintain that the church is too rigid, they forget what the word means; they imagine Catholics unthinkingly marching lockstep following orders from the hierarchy. Catholics have never been of one mind on any issue. When Catholics recite the Creed at Mass, they are probably announcing the only things that they agree about.

"Catholic" includes all—the lukewarm and the fervent, the observant and the nonobservant, the obedient and the intractable, the saint and the sinner. The very word *Catholic* implies inclusivity. Such comprehensiveness inevitably opens the way for disagreement and contradiction.

It has always been so. There was disagreement among the first Christians about whether the Gentile converts had first to become Jews (Acts 15). Paul, the Apostle of the Gentiles, argued against some of the converted Pharisees who insisted that Gentile converts be circumcised and required to keep the Mosaic Law. Peter sided with Paul and the face of the early church was radically altered.

On another occasion, Paul confronted Peter "to his face" when he thought that Peter "was clearly in the wrong." Peter, who had eaten with Gentile con-

Being Catholic

I always make the comparison to being Jewish — how do you stop being Jewish? I can't stop being Catholic in some way. I am totally formed in that tradition — and I like it. I like the help that it has given to me in thinking, even in thinking my way out of some of what it's taught me. I just don't give anybody a license to determine that. If you were doing an essay, you'd have to write your way around the contradictions in this because authority is certainly part of the tradition. But I think it has always been the case that everybody defined Catholicism for himself or herself, and there are millions and billions of Catholicisms running around embodied that don't fit the standard operating definition.[2]

–Robert Hoyt, Founding Editor, *National Catholic Reporter*

verts in opposition to Jewish law, refused to eat with them when he thought some Jewish converts were offended by his table sharing. Paul insisted that Peter could not have it both ways. Moreover, it is by faith in Christ, not by observance of the law, that everyone is justified (Gal: 2.11–21).

Another example of different theological and faith perspectives may be gleaned from the four Gospels. The writers give us different views of Jesus. Mark, for instance, presents an image of Jesus that focuses on his humanity. He speaks of Jesus' anger, sympathy and sadness. When criticized for curing on the sabbath, "He looked at them with anger"(3:5). In raising Jairus's daughter from the dead, he took the child by the hand and told them to give her something to eat (5:35–43).

Matthew reports that Jesus was sad in the Garden where he was betrayed; Luke has an angel comfort him; but Mark says simply that he was filled with fear and distress (14:34).

John's Gospel, on the other hand, is highly theological. He speaks of the Cosmic Christ who was present at the beginning. "In the beginning was the Word; and the Word was with God and the Word was God. He was in the beginning with God. All things came into being through him and without

What Does Being a Catholic Mean to You?

You might discover something about what the Catholic Church means to you if you complete the following sentences from the survey reported in *U.S. Catholic*:

I knew how much the Catholic faith meant to me when…
One thing that tries my Catholic faith is…
I am proud to be a Catholic because…
The most important Catholic tradition that should be passed on to our children is…
One thing Catholics do better than anyone else is…
It's evident that I'm Catholic because…
What I most appreciate about the Catholic faith is…
If I were to make a commercial for the Catholic Church, I'd be sure to mention the following highlights…[1]

him not one thing came into being" (1:1–3).

Throughout history, great theologians often disagreed, even as they do today. St. Thomas Aquinas and St. Bonaventure, who lived at the same time, developed theologies that were at odds with each other. Bonaventure, a monk, produced a devotional theology that reflected the monastic life. Thomas wrote from the perspective of the university. He was a schoolman, a scholastic who revolutionized theological methodology. Each taught from the perspective of his own context; it was inevitable that they interpreted theology differently.

Ours, then, is not the first generation to take advantage of the broad, inclusive nature of the Catholic Church.

We do not have access to what ordinary Christians of the past believed, but what is available to us suggests a diversity not unlike what we experience. History gives us some insight into what powerful leaders and significant thinkers of past ages did and said, but, for the most part, it does not provide clear clues about the vast majority of persons.

Defined by the Law

In spite of what has been said, it is easy to define who is a Catholic. Canon Law states that by baptism persons are incorporated into the church and remain so unless they formally join another denomination or publicly renounce a dogma of faith. The first is called apostasy and the second heresy. It is important to pay attention to all the words in the description of who is Catholic. To be officially outside the church would require *formal* acceptance in another church or *public* renunciation of dogma, that is, of a doctrine that is held by the church with solemnity and proclaimed with highest authority.

Catholics do not lose membership in the church, then, by missing Mass, by not making their "Easter duty," by picketing the diocesan office, or by disagreeing with the pope on some issue. There are Catholics who cannot name their bishop and some who may find it hard to remember the pope's name. They are Catholic nevertheless.

I am not making a case here for a superficial

alliance with the church or for lax adherence to its teaching. I am merely reminding us that Catholics come in all sizes and shapes and that the majority of us who go by the name Catholic may have a somewhat loose relationship with the institutional church. That institution is, of course, the church, but what defines the institution — the hierarchical structure, Canon Law, rules and regulations — is not the whole story. Being Catholic is as much mystery as it is institutional affiliation.

There are Catholics — too many — who feel alienated from the church. They may be hurt or

Still a Catholic

…when I go to a regular church, I feel like a total freak. And so I'm constantly thinking that there's no place for me in the church — it's just that there's no place else for me to go if I want to have some sort of a religious life. I'm still practicing Catholicism, but I'm not sure the Pope thinks I am. …But there is still no place for me to go in the church. It's only because it is a potential source for me — and has been in the past in isolated moments — of such beauty that cannot be replicated in the secular context, that I sort of stay in.

At its best, the church is also a source of tremendous idealism and charity. It's a combination of the esthetic ideal and the ethical ideal, both of which, to me, have a kind of purity you don't find elsewhere. The best of what I consider Catholicism that I can feel touched by and touch combines esthetic and moral intensity, and an image of love and responsibility and beauty that feeds you and enables you to go on with it. But the reality of life in the church now has nothing to do with that.[3]

–Novelist Mary Gordon

angry about some real or imagined affront and find themselves unable to participate in the life of the local church. Some, it is true, have found a home in another denomination, but the majority of those persons still identify themselves in some way with the term *Catholic*.

Is There a Typical Catholic?

Is there such a thing as a typical Catholic? Can we find an average Catholic who represents the majority of Catholics? Formal surveys and informal conversations remind us that wide disagreement on some significant issues in the church makes that job almost impossible. Catholics are sometimes now spoken of as "selective Catholics" or "smorgasbord Catholics" who pick and choose what they will obey.

The researchers involved in the Notre Dame Study realize that their statistics might set the upper boundary on church leaders' authority. Some results from Gallup polls that indicate a smaller role for church leaders may set the lower boundary. One reason may be that Gallup interviewed self-identified Catholics, whereas the Notre Dame study focused on active parishioners, those we

might call practicing Catholics.

When asked which level of the church should primarily speak on the above issues, parishioners were willing to assign the broad issues such as war, poverty and race to the hierarchy. But as the issues became more personal (equal opportunity regardless of workers' sex and birth control), they were inclined to label it a matter of individual conscience.

What is significant about today's controversies is that, unlike some previous ages, there is not widespread disagreement on doctrine but rather on discipline. We don't find ourselves in situations like that of fourth-century theologian Gregory of Nyssa[4]. The interest of people in the theological debate about whether Jesus was truly divine or only a creature subordinate to the Father captured everyone's attention. Gregory said that if you went to the baker for a loaf of bread, he would give his opinion about the Father being greater and the Son being subject to the Father. Going to the butcher may have given rise to a different kind of conversation and an opposite opinion.

While they may have developed new ways of relating to the institution, Catholics are also seeking

Church Voices on Public Issues
Who Should Speak, in the Viewpoints of Parishioners

	Some levels of Hierarchy	Combination of hierarchy speaking, individual deciding	Individual conscience alone
Aid to poor countries	83 %	7 %	10 %
Eliminate poverty from U.S.	83	8	9
Action for world disarmament	75	9	16
Racial integration	64	10	26
Sex, violence on TV	61	11	27
Equal opportunity regardless of workers' sex	56	7	38
Birth control	45	8	47

Notre Dame Study of Catholic Parish Life #11, 1987

new ways to live out their faith. John Coleman[5] has identified three changes that describe this new breed of Catholics. First, their affiliation with the institution is more selective even as they nurture Catholic social and communal ties. Second, they seek personalized experiences of community in new religious models such as the charismatic movement, scripture sharing groups, or small Christian communities. Third, they are likely to be involved in voluntary, nondenominational associations such as Bread for the World, the Peace Corps, or the Movement for Responsible Investment.

Practicing Catholics

The church exists to enable members to claim the splendor of the tradition, to celebrate the sacraments, to proclaim the gospel by their words and deeds, to enrich and be enriched by the community, and to assume responsibility for the transformation of the world. Previous remarks about the inclusive nature of the Catholic Church ought not to be taken as suggesting that a Catholicism that eliminates any of these characteristics is either the norm or the ideal.

Catholics who have opted out of full and vibrant membership may be likened to doctors and lawyers who, for whatever reason, no longer practice their profession. A doctor or lawyer who no longer practices is still a doctor or lawyer, but the profession no longer has the same influence on how they live and relate, how they make judgments and decisions. So non-practicing Catholics are still Catholic, but it may be difficult to recognize that by their lives.

Catholics for whom the church is central in their lives are often referred to as "practicing Catholics." Like practicing lawyers and doctors, their membership in the church affects all facets of their lives. True vital membership in the church demands that they know what the church teaches, that they celebrate its achievements and mourn its failures, that they are involved in the life of the local church.

To be Catholic in the full sense of that word is to love and reverence the church and to mourn when it fails to be all it could. To be Catholic is to be committed to the tradition and to know and hold fast to the doctrines taught. To be Catholic is to be convinced of the triumph of grace over sin and to be on fire with love for God and for the wonders of God's creation.

To be Catholic in the full sense of the word is a challenging and wondrous adventure.

Some Points of Disagreement

The points of disagreement among Catholics (even the most devout practicing Catholics) focus, for the most part, on two issues: the official church's statements on sexuality and those on the economy and war. On the one hand, some claim that the church has no right to interfere in what happens between spouses in their bedroom. On the other, some claim that the church has no right to criticize capitalism and the proliferation of nuclear arms. Some Catholics disagree with both positions.

Surveys indicate that about 87 percent of Catholic couples practice birth control, the vast majority not depending on the church-approved Natural Family Planning. Fewer than 12 percent of the Catholic population accept the birth control teaching reiterated by Paul VI in his 1968 encyclical *Humanae Vitae*.

Although the percentages today are greater, Catholics of the past were not necessarily in agreement with the official teaching either, nor did Catholic couples avoid using some sort of fertility control. A 1963 poll indicated that only 50 percent of American Catholics agreed with the church's teaching at that time. The development of safer and more convenient methods of birth control has had its impact on Catholic family planning as it has on persons of other denominations. Surveys also indicate that when women become more educated, they are likely to have smaller families.

The Notre Dame Study on Parish Life found that so-called "core Catholics" are as likely as nonpracticing Catholics to make up their own minds. "If they agree with the church on an issue, it is because the church position makes sense to them and they actively decide to agree. If the church teaching does not make sense to them, they will refuse to agree, no matter how often or how clearly or how authoritatively the church has spoken on it."

Issues concerning sexuality are not the only or even the most important ones that divide Catholics. The prophetic statements of American bishops concerning war, the economy, and poverty have angered and alienated some of the faithful. In their pastoral letter *Economic Justice of All* the bishops stated that "the obligation to provide justice for all means that the poor have the single most urgent economic claim on the conscience of the nation." Their criticism motivated a group of prominent conservative Catholics to write their own document upholding the free-market system as the most moral economic approach.

It is one thing to disagree with particular teachings of the church; it is another to maintain that the church has no right to interfere in certain issues. In both cases mentioned here — those who think that the church has no right to speak about contracep-

tion and those who think it has no right to speak about political issues — the point of disagreement is the same. It springs from a narrower definition of religion than that which is operating in the Institution.

Religion has been privatized to such an extent that many Americans do not think that religion — any religion — has a public role. The Notre Dame study identified 39 percent of Catholics as individualistic in the most deeply-held values that determine other beliefs. While 18 percent were exclusively communal in their foundational beliefs and 21 percent integrated individual and communal values, some 22 percent were unable to identify their religion in the terms used in the study. In spite of the fact that the church emphasizes communal symbols and rituals, the individualistic tendencies of the American persona affects how many Catholics view their religion.

But religion is not just about a spiritual and personal relationship with God; it is about how that relationship colors and shapes the whole of our lives. Religion is not only about worshipping on

The American Bishops on the Economy

This vision of economic life cannot exist in a vacuum; it must be translated into concrete measures. Our pastoral letter spells out some specific applications of Catholic moral principles. We call for a new national commitment to full employment. We say it is a social and moral scandal that one of every seven Americans is poor, and we call for concerted efforts to eradicate poverty. The fulfillment of the basic needs of the poor is of the highest priority. We urge that all economic policies be evaluated in the light of their impact on the life and stability of the family. We support measures to halt the loss of family farms and to resist the growing concentration in the ownership of agricultural resources. We specify ways in

which the United States can do far more to relieve the plight of the poor nations and assist in their development. We also reaffirm church teaching on the rights of workers, collective bargaining, private property subsidiarity and equal opportunity...

We believe that the Christian view of life, including economic life can transform the lives of individuals, families, schools and our whole culture. We believe that, with your prayers, reflection, service and action, our economy can be shaped so the human dignity prospers and the human person is served. This is the unfinished work of our nation. This is the challenge of our faith...

Economic Justice for All: Catholic Social Teaching and the U.S. Economy, 1986

Sunday but about how the rest of the week is spent. Thus religious leaders have the right and the duty to offer guidance about issues that confront Christians. And the faithful have the duty to listen respectfully and to study and weigh the words carefully. Then it is their duty to follow their conscience.

In the light of the findings of their poll of the American Catholic people, George Gallup and Jim Castelli assert that bishops have implicitly accepted "widespread dissent as the cost of continued unchallenged acceptance as members of the Catholic family." They suggest that the bishops have two choices in the face of widespread selectivity: discipline the dissenters or accommodate to the situation. Gallup and Castelli imply that the bishops have chosen to avoid substantial disruption on the part of a great number of Catholics.

We have been talking about the difficulty involved in defining the "typical Catholic." A recent study of American Catholics focused instead on who is a "good Catholic" (See box below).

This, of course, does not mean that the persons involved in the study are right, but it does provide insight into how Catholics perceive what membership in the church entails. Dissent is not to be taken lightly. It is the duty of Church leaders to provide guidance for the faithful, and it is the duty of each Catholic to develop a critical conscience, to heed the advice of the hierarchy, to pray for guidance, and to come to as honest a decision as possible. Neither blind obedience nor uninformed rejection is an appropriate response.

Communal Catholics

[Communal Catholics] are loyal to the Catholic collectivity and at least sympathetic toward its heritage. At the same time they refuse to take seriously the teaching authority of the leadership of the institutional church. Such communal Catholics are Catholics because they see nothing else in American society they want to be, out of loyalty to their past, and they are curious as to what the Catholic tradition might have that is special and unique in the contemporary world.[6]

–Andrew Greeley

Can a Person Be A Good Catholic Without Performing These Actions?
(Percentage saying yes)

Without going to church every Sunday	70%
Without contributing money annually to the special collection for the pope (Peter's Pence)	68%
Without obeying the church's teaching regarding birth control	66%
Without going to private confession at least once a year	58%
Without obeying the church's teaching regarding divorce and remarriage	57%
Without receiving Communion during the Easter time	53%
Without getting married in the church	51%
Without believing in the infallibility of the pope	45%
Without donating time or money to help the poor	44%
Without obeying the church's teaching regarding abortion	39%

American Catholic Laity in a Changing World[7]

Points of Agreement

Are there any points of agreement on what it means to be Catholic? Each one may come up with a different list and everyone might not use the same language that I do, but I would suggest that to be Catholic means to have a sense of the sacramental, to cherish celebration, and to relate to the saints, canonized or not, who have walked the road before us and who are still concerned for us.

Sacramental

The sacramental system has tattooed itself onto the

We are a Sacramental People
Notre Dame Magazine

Catholic character; we are a sacramental people, a people given to searching for and finding God in the persons, things, and events of everyday life. The major events of life are celebrated and ritualized and thereby lifted up and transformed. They become manifestations of God's presence with us — sacraments in which God's self-communication

Blessing of the Fields
Catholic News Service

(grace) is tangible and present in the sign.

We ritualize receiving persons into the community in the rites of initiation: Baptism, Confirmation, and Eucharist. We ritualize human love in the sacrament of Marriage. Leadership and ministry in the community are ritualized in the sacrament of Orders. At a time of illness or critical injury the Sacrament of the Sick sustains us. Each of the seven sacraments is a celebration of what the Christian community commits itself to as we share life in Christ. Each is the ritualization of what it means to live as a Catholic.

Sacramentality is rooted in a belief that all of creation is sacred. At each point in the myth of creation from the book of Genesis, God looked at what was created and saw that it was good. Catholics use the things of the earth not only because they are good but to remind us that the earth is permeated with the loving presence of God.

We use branches of trees, water, incense, candles, and ashes to remind us that God has saturated our universe with the Divine Presence. We use the things of the earth to remind us of our relationship with God. The invisible transcendent God is disclosed to us through the cosmos. The mysterious elements of creation are capable of making us aware of the presence of God. There is not a person, place, or thing that God cannot use to remind us that we are graced.

More than that, we take gifts of the earth and transform them through human efforts so that they may become the very Body and Blood of Christ. We pray at each Eucharist, "Blessed are you, Lord, God of all creation.

THE SACRAMENTS AND GRACE

The sacraments do not *cause* grace, in the sense that the redemptive grace of God in Jesus Christ is otherwise unavailable. The offer of grace is already present to the individual, to the church, and to the human community at large in God's original self-communication... The sacraments shape and focus that communication of grace so that the divine presence may be effective for this individual or for this group insofar as they are members of the Church and responsible for its mission.[8]

–Richard McBrien

Through your goodness we have this bread to offer which earth has given and human hands have made. It will become for us the bread of life... Through your goodness we have this wine to offer, fruit of the vine and work of human hands. It will become our spiritual drink." Through human work, grapes and wheat become something they were not — bread and wine — so that they may then become Christ present in the Eucharist. God is present in the things of creation and in the transformation of that creation by women and men.

Sense of Celebration

In a recent issue of *U.S. Catholic*, Catholics were surveyed about the importance of the church in their lives. On the question of what Catholics do better than anyone else, all the respondents mentioned that we celebrate better than anyone else. Responses included "Ceremony — the Easter Vigil Mass is our greatest example of this," and "Ritualize basic beliefs so beautifully and meaningfully," and even "Put up with poor liturgies when the liturgical ministers involved are trying with a sincere heart."

Protestant Martin Marty claims that Catholics "never feared the ecstasy of the dance," as have some Protestants. In fact, Catholics have been criticized for being overly earthy, sensual, carnal, even bawdy.

We are a people who know how to celebrate. Mardi Gras could only have developed in a Catholic city. In spite of the excesses, the event is a Catholic celebration of life. The elaborate costumes, the floats, the throwing of beads and doubloons, the music — all proclaim that life as given by God is good.

At midnight on Shrove Tuesday, after the revelry, a sentry walks the streets proclaiming that Lent has begun. The festivity is over. Another Catholic moment has begun.

I am not suggesting that Mardi Gras is the most appropriate ceremony to usher in Lent, but observing that it took a Catholic imagination and vision for it to develop.

The same may be said of the street fairs celebrating the feasts of St. Anthony or St. Gennaro. In cities lucky enough to have a large Italian population, these feasts mean parades carrying a statue of the saint through the neighborhood, games, good food and drink, and wide-open churches where prayers are offered and reconciliation effected in the midst of the festivities.

The St. Patrick's Day parade, especially in cities like New York, has become an interracial, international collection of Catholic groups who are celebrating their Catholicity if not their Irish background. The official stop at St. Patrick's Cathedral by high school bands, college students, police officers and fire fighters witnesses to the vibrancy of the church of the people.

The lavish colors, music, and dance of Hispanic fiestas are the spillovers from the church rituals of that community. Processions with statues and images almost always accompany the fiesta.

Festivities that are rooted in the Catholic ethos tend to be noisy, somewhat sloppy, a bit disorderly and chaotic, and even border on the raucous. But, at their best, they celebrate the wonder of a lavish

God who has provided so much to gladden us and the delights of life lived in community.

All celebrations pale before the central ritual of the Eucharist. When Catholics draw together to celebrate Eucharist, they are not putting on theater, reenacting the Last Supper. They are celebrating the real presence of Jesus among them in the community, in the presider, in the proclamation of the word and in the sacred meal that is shared.

Unfortunately, this same sense of celebration, this hunger for ritual, has left many Catholics dissatisfied with liturgy as celebrated in some parishes and has given rise to the fairly new phenomenon of parish-hunting, in which people search for a parish where liturgy is alive and nourishing. This is not to suggest that Christ is not present in all the celebrations of the community when it gathers for Eucharist, but simply indicates that the changes in the liturgy have given birth to a more particular kind of Catholic.

Communion of Saints

Theologian Avery Dulles, S.J., has said, "Hardly any practice is so distinctively Catholic as the cult of the saints."[9] "Saint" has come to refer to women and men who are united with God in heaven. But it has a richer meaning that includes all who profess faith in Jesus Christ. Paul refers to those who are "called to be saints" (1 Cor. 1:2; Rom. 1:7). One metaphor for the church is the Body of Christ; another is Communion of Saints. They are complementary and interrelated metaphors describing the same reality from different perspectives.

When Catholics speak of the Communion of Saints, they mean the relationship among the saints in heaven, the saints in purgatory and the saints on earth. Catholics talk over problems with their favorite saints in heaven, begging them to plead before the throne of God for them, and they expect the saints to care for them and hear their prayers.

They also pray and offer the Eucharist for those saints who are in purgatory. Purgatory is not a place. It is not full of fire and brimstone. It is a metaphor used to describe the pain and suffering of not being fully united with God. Purgatory is the way we describe a process whereby saints who have died may surrender their self-centered selves and be able to become one with God. It is a "second chance," of sorts.

Recognizing one another as saints may, at times, be more difficult. But belief in the Communion of Saints assures us that other persons who struggled to live their faith are united with God, in spite of human failures and sins. The common humanity we share with saints in heaven and purgatory encourages us when we discern our own sinfulness or that of the other saints we meet.

The church has proclaimed Mary under the title of the Immaculate Conception as the patron saint of the United States. While the words of Genesis 3:15 about enmity between the woman's seed and the serpent and the crushing of the serpent's head by her heel do not apply specifically to Mary, artists have depicted Mary as the Immaculate Conception crushing the head of the serpent, the symbol of evil.

A Litany of Saints

For all the saints
    who went before us
    who have spoken to our hearts
    and touched us with your fire,
    we praise you, O God.

For all the saints
    who live beside us
    whose weaknesses and strengths
    are woven with our own,
    we praise you, O God.

For all the saints
    who live beyond us
    who challenge us
    to change the world with them
    we praise you, O God.[10]

–Janet Morley

Carol Frances Jagen, B.V.M., in her book *Mary According to a Woman* suggests that the Immaculate Conception as patron of our country could not only function in an individual, personal way but also could assume more public significance and thus be able to move America to shoulder more responsibility for justice and peace around the world. Jagen asks whether this symbol of human freedom victorious over sin may serve as a call to struggle for social justice. "Can the Immaculate Conception be our symbol of human freedom from the power of evil wherever it exists? Can the Immaculate Conception become a vital symbol of the power of God's love, freely accepted and operative in our lives? . . . New meanings for this symbol must be interiorized and made operative in the minds and hearts of people of faith, young and old."

Why Catholics Stay Catholic

Priest-sociologist Andrew Greeley tells a story about a time he appeared on the Phil Donahue show. Donahue asked, "Don't you think it would be better if all these dissenting Catholics left the church? Wouldn't it be better for everyone if only those who agreed with the pope remained Catholic?" After some parrying back and forth, Greeley

11

insisted that Catholics remain Catholics because they like being Catholic. They like ritual and ceremonies, they like blessings,and praying the rosary. They like Midnight Mass, Good Friday services, processions, pilgrimages, and May Crownings. They like bringing home palm on Palm Sunday, braiding it into crosses and setting it in a place of honor. They like having smudges of ashes from those palms on their foreheads on the next Ash Wednesday. They like devotions to the saints; but especially they like Mary.

There is a kind of "folk religion" about much of Catholic daily life. Never-known-to-fail novenas are the answer to problems and crises facing Catholics. Medals and scapulars are still a kind of insurance against evil in the minds of many. Miracles are prayed for and are expected. When they occur, they are grandly celebrated.

To say that Catholics stay because they like being Catholic doesn't mean that they are submissive. Catholics may disagree with the pope on certain issues, but they like having a pope; they like, love, and respect the papacy. The papacy is viewed as a strong spiritual and moral force in the world. They may at times disagree with the pope, but there is no talk of things being better without a pope.

The symbols, art, and stories that are infused into the Catholic psyche have more holding power than statements of formal doctrines. The majority of Catholics are not affected very much by controversies among theologians or between theologians and the Vatican. They are not overly concerned about most statements from Rome. It is the Catholic sense of the sacred that holds Catholics.

Conclusion

This chapter is the background and the basis for all that follows. In subsequent chapters we will address the effects of the Second Vatican Council, changes in the role of laity and clergy, and major issues facing the church. Most of what will be said will be of vital interest only to a small proportion of Catholics. Most know about the Council because of transformations and modifications in the furniture of the local parish church. Few have read or studied the documents of the Council; what they know is what the secular press reported. But we have to keep in mind that they are the majority of those we call Catholic.

We celebrate their presence among us and rejoice in their contributions. It is not necessary to study theology to be Catholic; it is not necessary to play a public role in the parish to be Catholic; it is not even necessary to join the community for weekly worship to be Catholic. Some might lament that; others see it as the bedrock strength of the church that calls itself "Catholic."

Notes

1. "How U. S. Catholic Readers Take Catholicism Personally," *U. S. Catholic*, May 1994, 31–36.
2. Peter Occhiogrosso, ed., *Once a Catholic* (Boston: Houghton Mifflin, 1987), 329.
3. Ibid., 74.
4. Quoted in Elizabeth Johnson, *She Who Is* (New York: Crossroad, 1992), 3.
5. John Coleman, *An American Strategic Theology* (Mahwah, N.J.: Paulist Press, 1982), 178.
6. Andrew Greeley, *American Catholics: A Social Portrait* (New York: Basic Books, 1977), 272.
7. William D'Antonio, James Davidson, Dean Hoge, and Ruth Wallace, *American Catholics in a Changing World* (Kansas City: Sheed and Ward, 1989).
8. Richard McBrien, *Catholicism* (San Francisco: Harper, 1994), 793–794.
9. Avery Dulles, *The Catholicity of the Church* (Oxford: Clarendon, 1987), 85.
10. Janet Morley, Bread for Tomorrow: Prayers for the Church Year (Maryknoll: Orbis Books, 1992), 135.

2

Discovering Our Catholic Roots

Any discussion about the church must take seriously the significance of tradition. As Catholics, we believe that God is revealed in many ways but in a special way in the scriptures and in the ongoing life of the church. To speak, then, of the church in the United States is to speak of what have we received from that tradition and what have we contributed. It is to hold us responsible for tradition.

Maybe it is a mistake to speak of tradition as a noun; better think of it as a verb — something active, dynamic, vigorous. Tradition is not some static possession that one generation passes on to the next, untouched and unchanged, like some fragile family treasure from a past age. It is more like the family myths and stories that are passed on from generation to generation, each one enriching and fortifying the original. The practices, disciplines, doctrines and dogmas that define the Catholic Church today were not known in their present form by earlier Christians. The church observed many fast days and days of abstinence for centuries; it mandated clerical celibacy only in the eleventh century; it declared marriage a sacrament in 1439. Neither

these nor any other developments sprang full-blown from some pen in the Vatican. The magisterium makes official statements on each issue only after prayerful reflection on the practice of the faithful and the contributions of theologians.

Even more basic and profound doctrines than the disciplines and practices just mentioned developed over time. The dogma of the Trinity evolved over almost three centuries; the divinity of Jesus was proclaimed by the Council of Nicea in 325 in the words we still proclaim at Eucharist: "God from God, Light from Light, true God from true God."

It was not until the eleventh century that Pope Benedict VIII officially inserted the word *filioque* (and the Son) into the Creed. Christians in the West had been using the formula for centuries to proclaim their belief that the Spirit proceeded from the Father and from the Son. The Eastern church refused to change the ancient creed promulgated by the Council of Constantinople and still teaches that the Spirit proceeds from the Father. The Immaculate Conception was defined in 1854 and the Assumption of Mary in 1950.

Each of these beliefs has a long history during

The Development of Doctrine

Every Catholic holds that the Christian dogmas were in the church from the time of the Apostles; that they were ever in their substance what they are now; that they existed before the formulas were publicly adopted, in which, as time went on, they were defined and recorded, and that such formulas, when sanctioned by the due ecclesiastical acts, are binding on the faith of Catholics, and have dogmatic authority…

Language, then, requires to be refashioned even for sciences which are based on the senses and the reason; but much more will this be the case, when we are concerned with subject-matters, of which, in our present state, we cannot possibly form any complete or consistent conception, such as the Catholic doctrines of the Trinity and the Incarnation. Since they are from the nature of the case above our intellectual reach, and were unknown until the preaching of Christianity, they required on their first promulgation new words, or words used in new senses, for their due enunciation; and since these were not definitely supplied by Scripture, or by tradition, nor for centuries by ecclesiastical authority, variety in the use and confusion in the apprehension of them, were unavoidable in the interval… Not only had the words to be adjusted and explained which were peculiar to different schools or traditional in different places, but there was a formidable necessity of creating a common measure between the two, or rather the three languages — Latin, Greek and Syriac.

–John Henry Newman

which theologians argued for or against, some fell into heresy, the faithful incorporated the beliefs into their prayers and liturgies, and the magisterium, taking all into account, declared various doctrines to be the official teaching of the church. The hierarchy does not act alone but is responsible for listening to the *sensus fidelium* — the sense of the faithful. When we say, "The church teaches…" we mean just that — all of us. The whole church teaches, not just the bishops and the pope. This is not to deny the role of the hierarchy but to recall that church and hierarchy are not synonyms.

This discussion of the development of doctrine is meant to remind us that tradition is not some static deposit of wisdom and knowledge that is simply passed down untouched through the ages, but that each age is responsible not only for preserving but also for articulating the Tradition so that it remains vibrant and life-giving.

Of course, we do not have to struggle with pro-

The Deposit of Faith

Sacred tradition and sacred Scripture form one sacred deposit of the word of God, which is committed to the church. Holding fast to this deposit, the entire holy people united with their shepherds remain always steadfast in the teaching of the apostles, in the common life, in the breaking of the bread, and in prayers (cf. Acts 2:42, Greek text) so that in holding to, practicing and professing the heritage of the faith, there results on the part of the bishops and the faithful a remarkable common effort.

Vatican II, Dogmatic Constitution on Divine Revelation, 6

cessing beliefs about the nature of God and the divinity of Jesus, but we are responsible for educating ourselves about the issues of our day. We are a part of tradition. The church of the twentieth century has the right and obligation to preserve and reinterpret the myths, symbols, doctrines, and dogmas so that the church will flourish and remain living and vibrant. It is not a responsibility to be taken lightly; nor is it an excuse for individual acceptance or rejection of church teachings. We are a community that is traditioning. In community we come to learn what it means to be Catholic in this century.

This reflection on the development of tradition is both an introduction to a discussion of the church in the United States and an appeal for us to be involved in the questions and issues of our day that are determining the direction of the church for future generations. Catholics in the year 20,000 may look back at us and wonder how we of the early church articulated our faith.

A Rich Tradition

One problem with tradition is that we are inclined to romanticize it. Sometimes, as Catholics and as Americans, we long for the good old days when the citizens were more patriotic and Catholics more fervent. We recall Catholic explorers like Columbus, DeSoto, and Champlain, patriots like Washington, Jefferson, Adams, and Lincoln and we think, "They don't make them like that anymore." Compared to this century, the past (almost any time in the past) looks nearly perfect.

It may be hard for those of us given to nostalgia to admit that there never was a Golden Age, either in the church or in the country. Each age struggled with greater or lesser success to be faithful to the Christian message or to the foundational documents of this country as they responded to the demands of the time. Perhaps what we need is a quick look at history to appreciate the blessings and shortcomings of our own time and place as American Catholics. In this chapter, we will review some of the intertwined histories of church and state and attempt to uncover the theological principles and

religious beliefs that supported or challenged the life of our Catholic forebears. Given such a rich history and broad expanse of time and space that we are attempting to cover in a short space, it will be necessary to select certain important events and issues and omit others. Thus as we review our early history, we will focus on four topics: (1) the church and Native Americans, (2) Catholic and Protestant relationships, (3) internal issues, and (4) the relationship with Rome.

These topics, important in themselves, may provide significant insights as we face some of the significant issues today. Among these issues are inculturation, ecumenism, clergy-lay relationships, and the relationship of the church in the United States with the universal church. The way we address them is the way we will contribute to the tradition.

The Church and Native Americans

Columbus called his landing place San Salvador; significantly, he did not call it El Dorado (The Golden Place). When he planted the cross and the flag of Spain on the shore of the New World, he provided the symbols for the explorers and settlers who were to follow. The land and its people were claimed for the church and the Mother Country.

A devout Catholic, Columbus recorded the aims of his journey in his journal. One was to discover "the manner in which may be undertaken the conversion [of the natives] to our Holy Faith." Of course, another of Columbus's goals was to extend the power, wealth and prestige of Spain.

The salvation of souls and the accumulation of riches went hand-in-hand. And the responsibility for both these tasks lay with the laity as well as with the clergy. Note that Columbus's venture was a lay Catholic endeavor. There were no priests or religious on board. Columbus recited the Office daily and led the crew in prayer. It was this layman who claimed the land for El Salvador, the Savior.

Columbus Arrives in the New Land
Notre Dame Magazine

Europe at the time of the explorers. The 1992 celebration of the five-hundredth anniversary of Columbus's voyage reminded us how easy it is either to romanticize or to denounce the fervor of the explorers and settlers. Rather than judge them by the wisdom of this age, it may be better to try to understand the religious sensibilities of their time. Every school child knows the importance of the year 1492. Hardly anyone knows that in the same year, Ferdinand and Isabella routed the Moslems from Granada and expelled all Jews from the country in an effort to create a truly Catholic Spain. They believed, as did most others, that all unbaptized persons were condemned to everlasting pain and suffering. Baptism was absolutely necessary for eternal life. The monarchs had already reestablished the Inquisition, the primary purpose of which was to insure racial and religious purity. The Inquisition came to this continent in 1569 and was the most feared tribunal in the Spanish colonies.

It was in this repressive atmosphere that the New World was discovered and colonized.

Repressive as the events cited may be, the period of discovery also provides the witness of persons like Teresa of Avila, John of the Cross, Ignatius Loyola, and Thomas More. While Jewish and Moslem converts to Christianity were the chief victims of the Spanish Inquisition, Teresa and Ignatius were both suspects. During this difficult time in the church's history, women and men founded many religious orders to minister in schools, hospitals, jails and orphanages.

Given the variety of political and religious worldviews, it will come as no surprise that Europeans perceived the peoples who lived in this new land alternatively as noble savages or as heathens and pagans. In either case, they considered both the way of life and the Indians themselves as inferior to the cultured European lifestyle. Conversion to the Catholic faith and therefore to European customs was the order of the day. Martin Marty, Protestant historian of the Catholic Church, maintains that the first thing that the Indians had to give up was a positive view of their rituals, myths, traditions, and symbols.[1] The traditional religious motivation for their lives and for their relationships had to be disregarded. The abolition of their religion was necessary in order that they be saved through baptism. To this end, thousands of Franciscans, Dominicans, and Jesuits evangelized the natives at great cost, sometimes risking torture and their very lives.

Separation of state and religion was not yet a dominant value. Civil governments and religious institutions cooperated and supported one another's efforts; moreover, their goals often coincided. In 1493, Pope Alexander VI gave Spain the exclusive rights to evangelize the New World. Civil authorities had the right to appoint bishops and religious superiors, and to authorize the establishment of churches, monasteries, hospitals, and dioceses. Any church or pious institution built without the necessary permission was torn down.

Missionizing the Natives. Later, French and English missionaries and settlers followed the Spanish. The French settled in New France (now Canada) and Louisiana; the English, the northeastern part of what is now the United States. While the relationship of each group with the Indians was

colored by its national character, they all brought a zeal for the conversion of the people in the New World. When we consider the suffering and martyrdom that befell the missionaries, we might ask what motivated them. Were they better Christians than twentieth-century Christians?

I believe the answer is yes and no or even a resounding maybe.

In trying to understand human behavior, we do well to study motives. What impelled these people to risk everything in order to baptize the inhabitants of the New World? The theological understanding of the day suggested that the gospel promised salvation and heaven only to the baptized believers. The unbaptized were destined to hell. In an age that pronounced Jews and Moslems

Blessed Katherine Tekakwitha
Catholic News Service

Kateri Tekakwitha

Kateri Tekawitha, daughter of a Mohawk chief, is a candidate for canonization. She was born in what is now New York State. When she was very young, she lost most of her family during a smallpox outbreak that left her scarred. She learned about Christianity from the Jesuits but had to flee from her own people in order to follow Christ. She was baptized on Easter Sunday at the age of twenty and lived a life of prayer and charity in a Mohawk village in Montreal. She died four years after becoming a Christian and has been declared Blessed by the church.

damned to hell, it is understandable that the natives had to be baptized, no matter the cost.

Few questioned the prevailing theological insights of the time. But there were those few. Latin American missionary Bartolomeo de Las Casas, O.P., officially named protector of the natives by the pope, defined his role as one that began in crying for the suffering of the natives. Las Casas was able to see beyond the commonly held beliefs and courageously defended the people he saw being oppressed.

Although Las Casas is supposed to have said that it was no favor to save infants from hell and let them drown in the baptismal font, historians claim that he probably would have chosen baptism over a long life for a child.

It was difficult distinguishing between being Christianized and being Europeanized. The natives were schooled in European ways and taught to work for the good of the mission and the Crown. The lavish resources of their lands and the fruits of their labor became the treasure of the mother country.

Baptism often involved a whole new way of life for the natives: living at the mission, new clothes, food, work habits, leisure activities, and, in some cases, the breaking of polygamous marriages. But baptism did not always signify conversion of life. Part of the problem was trying to teach such doctrines as the Trinity without understanding the native languages and thought patterns. The Spanish thought the languages of the natives were not able to communicate the sacred truths. They therefore resorted to such things as the memorization of "Santisima Trinidad, Dios, Jesu Christo, Espirito Santo."

French missionaries did learn the language of the Native Americans with whom they worked. They had to be careful in the way they spoke of the Eucharist, avoiding any talk of the Body and Blood of Christ when speaking to tribes given to cannibalism. We have only to remember the circumstances of the martyrdom of the Jesuits Jean de Brebeuf, Gabriel Lalemant and Isaac Jogues to understand their predicament.

Despite the efforts of the missionaries, little is left of their efforts save a string of cities whose names testify to their faith: Santa Anna, San Francisco, San Diego, Santa Fe, Saint Augustine, to name but a few.

We have learned too late that respect for the culture and faith of a people is a prerequisite for any discussion about religion. In attempting to eliminate some of the beliefs of the Native Americans, European missionaries not only failed, for the most part, in their efforts at conversion, but they also impoverished themselves by not learning from a people who had a highly developed spirituality and belief system. The Native Americans' reverence for the earth and living in harmony with nature could have been one of their great gifts to the Europeans.

Even those who were converted accepted Christianity with a native flair. Christianity was colored by a determined adherence to their native religion. Traditional rituals, especially initiation rites, were not entirely abolished. The Great Spirit was recognized in the God whom the missionaries preached. It was not quite the brand of Christianity that was imported from Europe.

Catholic-Protestant Relationships

As more settlers came to these shores, attention shifted from evangelizing the natives to building the church among the pioneers. The conflicts between countries and religions in Europe were mirrored in the problems encountered in the new land. Catholic French and Spanish claims to the New World had been taken over by Protestant England.

Many came seeking religious freedom for themselves. People who believed something different deserved religious freedom also — but they should find somewhere else to practice it. English Protestants, remembering "Bloody Mary," the Catholic queen who preceded Elizabeth I, feared Catholics and, for the most part, were intolerant of them.

While much has been made of the tolerance of

Catholic colonies, especially Maryland, we do well to remember that Catholics were a very small minority and, in their efforts for tolerance, they may have been making a case for their own cause among the Protestant majority. The Act of Toleration, passed in 1649 in Baltimore declared, that no one in the province of Baltimore who professed belief in Jesus Christ should be in any way "troubled, molested or discountenanced for in respect of his or her religion nor in the free exercise thereof."

Remarkable for its time, the Toleration Act lasted only a few years. Puritan leaders gained power in Maryland, repealed the act, and outlawed Catholics in 1654. Thirty-eight years later, the Church of England was established by law in Maryland and Catholics were required to pay taxes to it and even, for a time, to attend services. In 1718, Catholics were completely disenfranchised, cut off from public life, denied the right to conduct schools, and restricted in their religious services. This situation lasted until the time of the Revolution.

On a happier note, Catholics were accepted in the Quaker colony founded by William Penn even when war between England and France made them suspects in a "popish plot."

Very little is known about Catholics in other colonies except New York. The English had captured New Amsterdam from the Dutch and named James, Duke of York, as proprietor of the renamed New York. James, a convert to Roman Catholicism, named Thomas Dongan, another Catholic, as governor. Dongan supported a bill of rights that guaranteed religious freedom for all citizens. Going beyond the protection insured by that bill, he once granted Sephardic Jews licenses to practice trade in New York. This experiment in toleration was as short-lived as the one in Maryland. In 1693, the Church of England was established in New York and religious toleration was not restored until 1806.

Among the founding fathers, only George Washington appears to have had any tolerance for Catholics. Samuel Adams was notoriously anti-Catholic, John Adams was not much better. Franklin, Jefferson, and other deists were suspicious of all revealed religions but of Catholicism in particular. Once when his troops were preparing to celebrate Guy Fawkes Day, Washington banned the burning of the pope in effigy (a practice celebrated by Protestants since Catholics were implicated in attempts to destroy the House of Parliament in 1605).

With the great wave of Catholic immigrants that began in early decades of the nineteenth century, concern about a papal takeover grew among some Protestants. Convents and churches were burned to the ground and street riots had religious as well as economic and political motivation.

Prejudice against Catholics showed itself with the establishment of the political party officially known as the American Party. Because of their usual answer when questioned about the purpose of the party they became known as the Know-Nothings. Know-Nothings railed against blacks and Catholics, promised to oppose the election of foreigners and Catholics to public office, and swore not to appoint Catholics to any political staff. The Know-Nothings were so much at odds with American ideals that they did not survive as a party.

In the late nineteenth century, respected journals like *Harper's Weekly* and *Atlantic Monthly* published cartoons and articles mocking Catholics, especially immigrant Catholics. One of the slogans in the presidential campaign of 1884 was that the Democratic party was the party of "rum, Romanism and rebellion."

Prejudice against Catholics was fired by fear. A rural association, the American Protective Society was able to foment trouble in 1893 by spreading a rumor that the pope had absolved all Catholics from allegiance to the United States. Catholics were supposed to be planning a wholesale massacre of heretical Protestants on September 5 which was erroneously believed to be the feast of Ignatius Loyola, founder of the Jesuits.

Whatever the reasons for the defeat of Alfred E. Smith's 1928 presidential campaign — and there were many — religion certainly contributed to it. Anti-Catholic fear and discrimination once more held the day.

Let us not think that Catholics were merely the victims of prejudice. Though in the minority, they fostered their own brand of intolerance. Protestants were seen as heretics and infidels who were to be avoided as threats to the faith. Catholic magazines and papers warned against Protestant values. The Catholic school system owes its development to fear of the Protestant culture that permeated public schools. Catholics lived, for the most part, in Catholic ghettoes, making it easier to obey the church's proscription against "mixed marriages."

This thumbnail history of religious intolerance helped to shape the Catholic Church in the United States in a siege mode, prepared for battle and ready to defend its beliefs and practices. Catholics, as a minority with a clearly defined enemy, clung defensively to their neighborhoods, customs, and faith.

In spite of what has been said about prejudice, and in spite of the legacy of Catholic and Protestant nations killing one another, of pogroms against Jews and Crusades against Islam, we, in this country, have never had a religious war. We have been able to establish a nation in which Christians, Jews and Moslems are striving to learn to live in peace with one another.

Internal Issues

Not all problems that faced the church in the beginnings of our country were from the outside,

---

The Know-Nothings

I am not a Know-Nothing. How could I be? How can anyone who abhors the oppression of negroes, be in favor of degrading classes of white people? Our progress in degeneracy appears to me to be pretty rapid. As a nation, we began by declaring that *"all men are created equal."* We now practically read it, "all men are created equal, *except negroes.*" When Know-Nothings get in control, it will read, "all men are created equal, except negroes, *and foreigners, and catholics.*" When it comes to this I should prefer emigrating to some country where they make no pretense of loving liberty — to Russia, for instance, where despotism can be taken pure and without the base alloy of hypocracy [sic].

–Abraham Lincoln

---

however. Because the New World was so unlike Europe, clergy and laity had to learn new ways of relating. The spirit of independence, the lack of formal structure in the church, and the paucity of clergy all contributed to the tension.

Who is to lead? For more than two hundred years, Catholics lived and died on this continent without the benefit of a bishop. It was not until 1790 that John Carroll was ordained first bishop of Baltimore. The ordination had to take place in Europe since there were no bishops in the United States. Six years before, Carroll had been named superior of the American Catholic missions and as such was under the jurisdiction of the Propaganda, the Vatican congregation in charge of missions. The clergy, especially Jesuits who had had their order suppressed by the Vatican in 1773, were unhappy about this situation. What was needed, they thought, was a bishop who would be accountable to the pope and not to a Vatican congregation. The democratic spirit alive among the clergy is evident in their request to elect the bishop rather than have one appointed by Rome. Carroll wrote that the appointment by a foreign tribunal "would shock the political prejudices of this Country."

This democratic impulse was short-lived. At first, Carroll consulted priests about the appointment of bishops, then selected bishops for Boston, Philadelphia, and Bardstown, Kentucky himself.

Finally he had to accept an Irish bishop for New York appointed by the pope without any consultation in the United States. The new bishop had been recommended by the Irish hierarchy.

Jay Dolan,[2] historian of Catholic America, maintains that the bishop and clergy missed an opportunity to shape the Catholic Church in America according to democratic principles. Carroll and twenty-two priests held a synod in 1791 and adopted the same laws that had been issued in earlier European synods. The documents they drew up were more in accord with the long tradition of European Roman Catholicism than with the republican spirit of the United States. Perhaps it is too much to demand that late-eighteenth-century clergy might have foreseen an alternative model that could be as faithful and loyal to the church as the one they were accustomed to.

Be that as it may, the spirit of independence and republicanism did have their effects on the life of the church. This is especially evident in the relationship between the laity and the clergy.

What of the laity? History is often associated with dates and names of great leaders of wars or governments. But history is also about the lives of people in particular circumstances and about their response to those circumstances. In this section we will discuss the role of the laity in the building of the church in America. There are no great names recorded, but historians have been able to draw a picture of the efforts of the pioneer Catholics to build the church on these shores.

Persistent problems for Catholics in the seventeenth and eighteenth centuries were the shortage of priests and the vast area over which Catholics roamed. In 1790, nine-tenths of the population lived on farms and the six largest cities were home to only three percent of the population. Five years before that date, Bishop Carroll reported that there were 25,000 Catholics and twenty-four priests in America. Two of the priests were over seventy and three others a few years younger. Of course, communication being what it was, Carroll could not have known of the number of Native American Catholics or of the French Catholics in Canada. What he knew was the state of the church in the original thirteen colonies.

Greatly outnumbered by Protestants and widely scattered, Catholics could not depend on the church they knew in Europe. There were no cathedrals, nor country churches, nor even wayside chapels. There were no town squares about which neighborhoods grew. There were few or no resident priests. It was, in large part, the responsibility of the lay women and men in the church to insure the survival of the faith.

As the frontier pushed westward, Catholics united, bought land, built a church, conducted services, catechized the children, and elected men to assume responsibility for the religious life of the community. The celebration of the Eucharist was infrequent; baptisms, marriages, and funerals were conducted by the laity, even as happens today in some remote areas of Latin America and Africa.

There was virtually no hierarchical structure as such — recall that there was no bishop for two hundred years — nor any formal organization into parishes and dioceses. The hierarchical system Catholics had left behind in Europe seemed out of place here. The spirit of democracy, republicanism, and independence affected the way people related to all facets of their lives, including the church. The example of their Protestant neighbors encouraged them to create communities and benevolent societies for the preservation of their faith.

In the process, a basis for lay trusteeism grew. As parishes began to develop, trustees were elected to continue the work that laymen had done in the absence of priests. Trustees were men who paid a pew tax and who were empowered to govern the parish in temporal affairs. These congregational parishes were democratic and treasured their autonomy. In this, they were not unlike the Protestant parishes that were growing at the same time.

The concept of lay trusteeism was supported by the clergy at first. But problems arose when, in some parishes, trustees assumed the right to hire and fire priests. For instance, in 1787, a group of German Catholics in Philadelphia had themselves incorporated and established the first national parish in Holy Trinity Church. When they attempted to hire a German-born priest, Bishop Carroll intervened, but to no avail. The congregation was declared in schism and it was fifteen years before the controversy was settled and the schism healed.

In New York, in response to an appeal from Archbishop John Hughes, all but one parish, St. Louis in Buffalo, gave up their civil right to hold church property. Hughes put the parish under interdict and excommunicated all the trustees. The parishoners at St. Louis managed to get a law passed that upheld trusteeism. The Putnam Bill forbade ownership of church property by clergy. While it was never enforced, it was repealed only at the outbreak of the Civil War, when civil leaders realized that Catholic support for the war depended upon the advice of their clergy.

Feelings were strong both for and against trusteeism. In St. Mary's parish in Philadelphia a twenty-year feud erupted in a riot in which parishoners with bats and bricks injured more than one hundred other parishoners.

Conflicts like this led historians to describe trusteeism in negative terms until very recently. More contemporary historians see in the system of lay trustees the seed of the involvement of the laity in the church today.

The immigrant church/es. One of the definitions that the dictionary gives for the word *Catholic* is "all inclusive." The history of the Catholic Church in the United States in the nineteenth century is both an example of and a test of that inclusivity. Millions of immigrants who arrived from Ireland, Germany, Italy, and Poland (and in lesser numbers from other European countries) identified themselves as Catholic and affirmed the Catholicity of the other

Pioneer Chapel
Notre Dame Magazine

national groups. They knew that no one nation or people could claim the title exclusively.

But, while they shared the same doctrines, sacraments and allegiance to the pope, their customs, practices, rituals, and history set them apart from one another. Settling in cultural ghettoes, the various nationalities had little to do with one another. Ethnic prejudices and suspicions as well as pride in one's own tradition separated Catholic from Catholic.

The establishment of national churches insured that the language, customs, and values of the old country would be preserved. German Catholics, especially, took responsibility for the establishment of their own churches and schools. Lay leaders organized the people, raised money and built a church, and then petitioned the bishop for a priest. In 1844, a group of German Catholics in Cincinnati held an organizational meeting, elected a building committee of ten men, drafted a constitution that was ratified by the community, bought land in the name of the bishop, and voted to name the parish St. John the Baptist. They voted on how much

Mother Cabrini

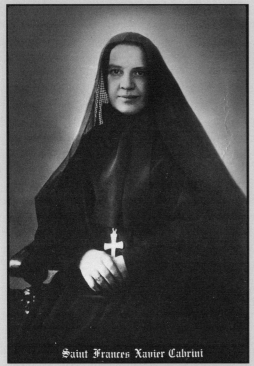

Saint Frances Xavier Cabrini

Mother Frances Cabrini
St. Francis Cabrini Shrine

Mother Frances Xavier Cabrini arrived in New York in 1889. She founded the Missionary Sisters of the Sacred Heart to minister to poor Italian immigrants. On fire with the zeal of her patron saint, she and her sisters established schools, hospitals, and orphanages. Cabrini crossed the ocean thirty times, making friends for the people she served and raising money for her projects. She became a citizen of the United States in 1909 and died eight years later. In 1946, Mother Cabrini became the first American citizen to be canonized.

money to spend, how many doors to build, how thick to make the walls, and what size to make the windows. In March 1845, the people planned the ceremony, procession, and celebration for the laying of the cornerstone. The system of lay trustees was very strong in German parishes.

Irish Catholics did not develop their parishes in quite the same way, for two main reasons: The clergy in the New World spoke their language, and Irish Catholics were more dependent on the clergy. Ordinarily, they petitioned the bishop for a priest who then took responsibility and leadership for the building of a church. The Irish were not passive and submissive, however; they too had a system of lay trustees, but the role of the clergy was more clearly defined.

Great numbers of Italian immigrants arrived a generation after the Irish and Germans and had an altogether different relationship with the institutional church than either of the other two groups. While religion was a major force in their lives, they were not given to frequent Mass attendance. Because of their experience of the church in Italy, they arrived with a heightened anticlerical streak. Italians were unique in that they established mutual benefit societies like the ones they knew back home. These societies contributed to the economic and social good of the new immigrants. They also were the means by which Italian Catholics were able to establish parishes for themselves.

Italians settled in large cities as did the Irish before them. At first, efforts were made to accommodate them into parish life, but the "Italian Mass" was often celebrated in the church basement or at odd times. Feeling like second-class citizens in Irish parishes, they soon established Italian national parishes.

Poles and other Eastern Europeans followed and established neighborhoods and parishes, experiencing much the same internal conflict with other ethnic Catholics. The church neglected the mission churches of an earlier century and the Mexican immigrants who settled there. The Southwest was no-priest land and, as a result, a folk-religion Catholicism grew with religious festivals, processions, and devotions to saints as more central than parish involvement. When clergy finally did arrive, the majority of them were French with little appreciation of Spanish culture. Some of the Romanesque architecture stands witness to the conflict between the Hispanic religious experience of the people and that of the clergy.

Speaking in general of Irish, Germans, Italians, Poles and Mexicans may give the illusion that all or most were involved in parish affairs. There are indications in church archives that no more than 50 percent of Catholics attended church regularly, and probably only about 25 to 30 percent formed the core of regular churchgoers. At the same time, all Catholics identified themselves in some way with the parish. Neighborhoods were defined by the parish church. In some areas, they still are.

Spiritual life of the people. It is not enough to study the leaders of wars, governments, and movements to understand history; it is not even enough to study the political and public involvement of ordinary people in these events. Careful attention also needs to be paid to the personal life of a people to understand history. When discussing the history of the church, we look to the leaders, and to the participation of the laity in the public church life, but we also need to investigate the inner, personal religious lives of the people.

The spirituality that developed in the nineteenth and early twentieth centuries may best be described as devotional.

In the early 1800s, churches and devotions were plain and spare. Missionaries, used to the grand edifices of Europe, wrote home about the lack of beauty in church architecture and decorations. There was only one altar, few if any stained-glass windows, statues, pictures, vestments, or sacred vessels.

As is often the case, the architecture and decorations symbolized the faith-life of the people. The simplicity of the outward structures was carried over to their devotional life. Sunday worship included Mass, Vespers, and Benediction when possible. Practices like the rosary were personal and private, not communal devotions. Sermons and pious books emphasized personal relationship with Jesus and the proper interior disposition, without which good works meant nothing.

In 1818, Jesuit John Grassi described a typical Sunday visit to a local church. After arriving by horseback, as did most of the congregation, the priest spent the morning hearing confessions, then celebrated Mass about noon. Sometimes the ser-

Circuit Rider Priests
Archives of the Congregation of the Holy Cross

Devotion to Mary
Archives of the Congregation of the Holy Cross

plainness and set about introducing more ornate decorations and buildings. The rise of Gothic and Romanesque churches in cities symbolizes a shift in American Catholic spirituality. The move from simple, plain churches to more ornate ones decorated with images, statues, and stained-glass windows accompanied the move to a devotional spirituality. As parishes grew more stable and the number of priests increased, practices that identified the post–Council of Trent church were adopted. Devotion to the saints, especially the Blessed Virgin, sometimes became more important than the Mass to some Catholics. The role of Christ in their lives seemed to be overshadowed.

Attention shifted from Sunday Mass to such devotions as the Nine First Fridays, Sacred Heart Novenas, and public recitation of the rosary. Among the most popular were Forty Hours Processions, adoration of the Blessed Sacrament, and Benediction, in which gazing at and adoring the host were emphasized.

A monumental shift in spirituality occurred once again when the theologians of the Second Vatican Council placed the celebration of the Eucharist at the center of Catholic practice and spirituality. While some of the devotional practices still exist, they do not hold center stage but are seen in the light of the communal celebration of the Eucharist.

mon had to be put off until after Mass to give him a chance to have a bite to eat. The afternoon was taken up with catechism classes for the children, baptisms, weddings, and the blessing of graves of congregants who had died. On Sundays when the priest was visiting other local churches, the people were encouraged to meet to read the prayers of the Mass or some instructions from a Catholic book.

Some missionaries did not appreciate such

Relationship between Rome and the Church in the United States

Americanism. The "phantom heresy" known as Americanism developed, in part, in opposition to this overly devotional spirituality. Convert Isaac Hecker, founder of the Paulist Fathers, called for a new spirituality that arose from the experience of American democracy. He focused attention on the work of the Holy Spirit in each individual soul and the responsibility of women and men to cooperate with the Spirit in renewing the face of the earth. While he supported the authority of the institutional church, he criticized passivity and docility. Obedience to external authority without internal commitment, he thought, was servile and unworthy of Christians.

A French translation of a biography of Hecker was eagerly accepted by Catholics who were trying to work out an accommodation with the new French Republic. But it also included an introduction that appeared to threaten the clergy who supported the monarchy. Hecker's work was criticized and found wanting by the standards of the *ancien régime*. The so-called heresies were summed up under the title "Americanism" and included such things as discounting contemplation in favor of action, valuing the natural over the supernatural, stressing the rights of the individual over ecclesiastical authority, and the idea that the church should adjust to modern science and knowledge.

These half-truths spurred Leo XIII to issue a condemnation of Americanism in 1899, explaining that these trends could impinge on the church's doctrine and moral standards. On the other hand, Leo wrote, "If indeed, by that name [Americanism] be designated the characteristic qualities which reflect honor on the people of America, just as other nations have what is special to them; or if it implies the conditions of your commonwealths, or the laws and customs which prevail in them, there is surely no reason why We should deem that it ought to be discarded."

With the convening of the Councils of Baltimore, American bishops began to develop a sense of collegial ties. The first council was in 1852, a time when tensions were rising between North and South. The second council was convened the year after the war ended. That meeting of the bishops

Isaac Hecker

The primary questions with us are the Trinity, the Fall and Hell. For our Protestantism is rapidly going over to Unitarianism, and this is fast becoming Universalism. These points must be thoroughly ventilated in order to meet the objections of intelligent non-Catholics. The work of our day is not so much to defend the church against the attacks of heresy, as to open the way for the return of those who are without any religion, true or false. We have to begin the conversion of these people *de radice*, and to do this in our day and civilization, theology requires to be entirely recast. This conviction has forced me to take a new standpoint from the start, and to bring it out on all occasions. [3]

–Isaac Hecker

Isaac Hecker
University of Notre Dame Archives

27

brought together men who supported opposite sides of the conflict. That they were able to address doctrinal issues as well as the situation of immigrants and the need for schools gives witness to the leadership that saw the need for a council to contribute to the healing process.

Civil War problems were not the only crises Catholics were facing. Tensions because of Vatican pronouncements added to the difficulties. Pius IX issued the Syllabus of Errors in 1864. The Syllabus condemned many things that Americans held dear, such as progress and modern civilization.

The doctrine of the infallibility of the pope was promulgated in 1870, against the advice of some American bishops who thought the timing was bad and that Protestants in the United States would misunderstand. It did help to shore up the authority of the pope and eventually of bishops and clergy. Fourteen years later, the Third Plenary Council of Baltimore declared the will of the bishop in local affairs supreme.

That, along with the end of the trustee system, helped the church in America move from a congregational model of church to a hierarchical one. Martin Marty suggests that Catholicism in America, given its history, could have developed along the lines of the low-church Protestant model, but it would no longer have been Roman Catholic. The loyalty of the American church to its Catholic tradition would have been well nigh impossible without some hierarchical structure.

Notes

1. Martin Marty, *An Invitation to American Catholic History* (Chicago: Thomas More Press, 1986), 31.
2. Jay Dolan, *American Catholic Experience: A History from Colonial Times to the Present* (Notre Dame: University of Notre Dame Press, 1992). This work has been a great help in the development of this chapter.
3. "Some Letters of Father Hecker," *Catholic World*, June 1906, quoted in Philip Gleason, *Keeping the Faith: American Catholicism Past and Present* (Notre Dame: University of Notre Dame Press, 1987) 160.

3

The Church in the United States Contributes to the Universal Church

Liturgical Renewal

One of the glorious characteristics of Catholicism is our sense of ritual. The pageantry of Christmas Mass, of Good Friday, of Easter Sunday, the striking symbolism of the sacramental system, the artistry expressed in vestments, music, and movement — all proclaim that in our liturgies we are celebrating our relationship with the Mystery that is our God. That dialogue with God takes on different accents in the various cultures in which the church finds itself. It is colored by each of the particular contexts in which the church lives. Inherited from our European forebears, the rituals that nourish faith are now marked by the American experience. In this section, we will discuss some of the contributions of the church in the United States to the recent liturgical movement.

It may be surprising to note that Charles Carroll, ordained the first American bishop in 1790, petitioned Rome to celebrate the Mass in English more than two centuries before that change was made. Although this request was denied, the idea did not die. It may also surprise us that English was commonly used during Mass and at other liturgies during Carroll's time. It was in 1810 that the American bishops decided to limit the use of the vernacular.

In the early years of the twentieth century, the use of the vernacular was among the issues resurrected by the forerunners of the liturgical movement in the United States and abroad. Their number was small and they did not represent the experience of most Catholics.

In the time before Vatican II, the spiritual life of most Catholics could be described as devotional. Benediction of the Blessed Sacrament and novenas in honor of Our Lady of the Miraculous Medal, St. Jude, and St. Anthony were ordinary staple in almost every Catholic parish. Devotion to the rosary was so strong that many Catholics prayed all fifteen decades every day. Private novenas honored saints for their specialties: Christopher for a safe journey, Anthony for lost objects, Jude for impossible cases,

Devotional Prayer Cards
University of Notre Dame Archives

and Gerard for a safe pregnancy and delivery were only a few among the many popular devotions. Many parishes continue such devotions in the mid–90's often under lay leadership and not nearly so well attended.

But Flannery O'Connor, that great Catholic writer, confided, "I hate to say most of these prayers written by saints-in-an-emotional-state. You feel you are wearing somebody else's finery and I can never describe my heart as 'burning' to the Lord (who knows better) without snickering."[1] It is said that artists are able to express the theology of a people about a generation before theologians find the words to describe it.

O'Connor certainly spoke for some whose hearts did not burn. Benedictine Virgil Michel was among that number. Michel recognized the profound connection between liturgy, community, and a just society. He invited Dorothy Day and Peter Maurin, founders of the Catholic Worker's Movement, to speak to the monks and help forge the connection between the way we pray and the way we live. Michel maintained that "we cannot give ourselves to God in God's own way, i.e., through Christ in his liturgical life, without becoming ardent apostles of social action."[2] As early as 1926, Michel began the publication of *Oratre Fratres*, now known as *Worship*, the principal American journal on liturgy.

Sometimes it seems as if some Catholics appear to believe that the Holy Spirit directs the workings of the church in some mysterious way, whispering into the ears of popes and bishops. The Holy Spirit acts today as in the past — in the lives of all who are attentive to the workings of the Spirit. Hard work on the part of Christians, prayer, and discussion precede any pronouncement by the institutional church. This, of course, does not guarantee that every pronouncement is correct or that it will not be changed at some future date. But it is a necessary component for the work of the church.

The extraordinary developments in the area of liturgy that resulted from the Second Vatican Council are the fruits of the planning, dreaming, work, research, discussions, and prayer of many persons in the decades before the council as they tried to be attentive to the voice of the Holy Spirit in the signs of their times. Small groups, sometimes unaware of one another, contributed in a variety of ways to the process of restoring the Eucharist to its central place in the life of the church.

Liturgical Pioneers

Musician Justine Ward, conscious of the poor quality of the music used in many churches, devised a method to teach Gregorian Chant to children. The Pius X School of Liturgical Music, established in 1916 by Ward and Mother Georgia Stevens, R.S.C.J., aimed at training teachers in the fine points of chant so that they could return to their schools and parishes and teach the next generations fine church music. Artists like Adé Bethune helped Catholics move from the somewhat saccharine art of the time with her contributions to the Catholic Worker and to *My Sunday Missal*. Bethune drew scriptural scenes but placed women and men in modern dress in them, helping Christians to make the profound connections between their own lives and the life of Jesus.

My Sunday Missal was the work of Father Joseph Stedman, a Brooklyn priest who wanted to "take the Big Book off the altar and put it into the hands of Catholics in the pew." This missal, first published in 1932, guided Catholics through the ordinary and proper parts of the Mass by the use of numbers and pictures. At a time when the Mass was celebrated in Latin and the priest had his back to the congregation, this missal revolutionized the participation of Mass goers. It made them more participant than observer.

My Sunday Missal

A handful of Benedictine monks who at first came together to discuss liturgical issues decided to see if a Liturgical Week, like the ones held in Louvain, Belgium, would work in the United States. To their surprise, more than twelve hundred persons attended the first week in Chicago in 1940 and heard

what were then revolutionary ideas, such as renewing baptismal promises at Easter and focusing more attention on the baptismal font during the Easter season. It was at the 1964 Liturgical Week in St. Louis that the first Mass sung in English in the United States was celebrated.

Two encyclicals of Pope Pius XII gave impetus to the fledgling liturgical movement: *Mystici Corporis* and *Mediator Dei*. The first defined the church as the Body of Christ, helping Catholics move from a kind of individualistic spirituality to a more communal one. The second fostered liturgical renewal, especially the Holy Week liturgies.

Seven years after the first Liturgical Week, the University of Notre Dame began its summer sessions in liturgy. The program included not only classroom instruction but the celebration of the liturgical hours and Eucharist each day. Eventually, the program grew into one of the premier graduate programs in liturgy and contributed to the theological basis for liturgical renewal.

Virgil Michel's protégé, Godfrey Diekmann, was one of the *periti* or experts who advised the bishops at the Second Vatican Council and who helped craft the first document issued by the council, *The Constitution on the Sacred Liturgy*. The Benedictines have been recognized as important contributors to the liturgical movement in the English-speaking world. Diekmann, like so many others who finally made important contributions, was not invited to the first session of the council.

Vatican II's Constitution on the Sacred Liturgical

It has been said that there were more arguments about the document on the liturgy than about any others. At one point, bishops opposed to it had it removed from the agenda until a group led by Cardinal Albert Meyer of Chicago collected more than eight hundred signatures on a petition to have it reinstated. They had only one-half hour to get the job done. The pope had it put on the agenda for the next session.

Vatican II and Liturgical Renewal

The church, therefore, earnestly desires that Christ's faithful, when present at the mystery of faith, should not be there as strangers or silent spectators. On the contrary, through a proper appreciation of the rites and prayers they should participate knowingly, devoutly and actively. They should be instructed by God's word and be refreshed at the table of the Lord's body; they should give thanks to God; by offering the Immaculate Victim, not only through the hands of the priest but also with him, they should learn to offer themselves too. Through Christ the Mediator, they should be drawn day by day into ever closer union with God and with each other, so that finally, God may be all in all.

Constitution on the Sacred Liturgy, 48

Diekmann recorded his elation in his diary when, by a vote of 2,158 to 19 (with one invalid vote), the *Constitution on the Sacred Liturgy* was the council's first document passed on November 22, 1963. It was sixty years to the day since Pius X published his *motu proprio*, "Restoration of Sacred Music." The celebration that evening was tragically cut short with the announcement of the assassination of John F. Kennedy.

This thumbnail history of the workings of the Spirit in the church leading up to the liturgical reforms of the council is, of course, incomplete, but it does illustrate how doctrines and practices mature in the Christian community. Most often, what begins as the interest of only a small group is tested in the larger community and researched by theologians, scripture scholars, church historians, and liturgists. Those issues that stand that test are then brought to the hierarchy for official approbation. This pattern can also be seen in the development of social teachings regarding the economy, war, racism, and sexism, for instance.

As a result of document on the liturgy, dramatic changes were effected: The altar is turned around, the language of the people is used instead of Latin, the greeting of peace is restored, and lay women and men are able to serve as ministers to the worshipping community. But these are outward changes. The great development is the theology that underlies these changes.

Liturgical development would have been impossible without the renewed attention paid to the Mystical Body of Christ. When Christians take seriously that we are the Body of Christ the liturgical developments of the past fifty years make sense. The metaphor of the church as the Body of Christ and the universal call to all Christians to live a life of holiness enables us to understand liturgy as an act of worship on the part of the *community* — the community that is Christ's very Body. It is an action of that body, not the work of one person, that is observed by others.

Religious Liberty

If we have the wisdom and the temper to preserve [civil and religious liberty], America may come to exhibit a proof to the world, that general and equal toleration, by giving a free circulation to fair argument, is the most effectual method to bring all denominations of christians to a unity of faith.

–Bishop John Carroll

Moreover, each Eucharist is meant to unite the local community with the church universal. While we have come to realize that Eucharist is not the time for private prayer but for communal prayer, it seems that we have not fully realized that Eucharist is not just the coming together of the local Christian community, of people who are more or less alike: Eucharist is the bond that holds together the church universal.

Religious Freedom

America's greatest gift to the Catholic Church — that is how Vatican II's *Declaration on Religious Freedom* has been described. The principles of the Declaration of Independence and the Constitution of the United States became the grist for theological reflection on the meaning of freedom, individual rights and responsibilities, and the duty of the government to defend those rights.

Historical Background

The idea of the separation of church and state was one that the first bishop, John Carroll, addressed in the late eighteenth century. In the religiously pluralistic world of the post–Revolutionary War days, he sought to build a church that was independent from foreign influence and, at the same time, respectful of the faith of others.

About a century later, Bishop John England spoke of a free church in a free society. Because he understood the church more in terms of democratic principles than monarchical ones, he fostered the development of such practices as local church councils and the trustee system. Adaptation to the culture in which the church found itself was not universally accepted. Many thought that the church was and, by rights, should be unchangeable. But by the time of Vatican II, the idea of change and development was ready for more universal approval.

American bishops at the First Vatican Council introduced new ideas that challenged European traditions. They wanted to elect members to the rules committee rather than have them appointed; to have sufficient time to review the credentials of candidates for other committees; to have the right to introduce proposals. They thought the process would be improved if the committee meetings were open, if adequate press facilities were provided, and if they moved to a place where everyone could hear better. American bishops had more reservations about the proclamation of the doctrine of infallibility than most European bishops. Some left Rome before the vote so as not to have to vote against the pope.

John Courtney Murray

The contributions of Americans at the First Vatican Council (1869–1870) foreshadowed later America's role at the next council. Jesuit John Courtney Murray was able to express the American position on religious freedom in such a way as to provide strong theological bases — in such a strong way, in fact, that it became the official teaching of the church.

Murray is generally credited as the person most responsible for the theological groundwork that eventuated in the *Declaration on Religious Freedom*. As a young theologian, he appealed for a theology that focused on "the liveability of the Word of God." His ideas about religious freedom are evident in these early writings. He believed that religious freedom as practiced in the United States was compatible with Catholic teaching and that Christianity was a basis for the American belief in the dignity of the individual. Further, this dignity demanded freedom of conscience in each individual's relationship with God. He saw the separation of church and state as a means of protecting that right.

His work was opposed by some American as well as European theologians who believed that the ideal situation occurred when the state took care of temporal needs and the church spiritual ones. In this ideal situation, the Catholic Church would be the officially recognized religion; until that time, compromises had to be made. Religious freedom, they believed, was acceptable when the Catholic Church was in the minority, but in countries where Catholics were the majority, the government had the responsibility to support the church.

Murray also argued that the articulation of certain church teachings was outdated and some were based on obsolete concepts of authority. The duty of the theologian, he believed, was not to search for support for papal pronouncements but to express Christian truths in terms that were understandable to twentieth-century people. Murray did not propose rejecting Christian doctrine but rather making it easier to fathom. He called theologians to be historically sensitive, to be aware of how doctrines had developed in the past. He used the analogy of the seed which becomes a bud, then a flower, and finally a fruit.

Murray had been among those theologians who were silenced by Pius XII and not permitted to publish.

Vatican II

Like some other prophetic thinkers who had put forth controversial ideas, Murray was not invited to the first session of the council. But he was named a *peritus* (expert advisor) by New York Cardinal Francis Spellman for the subsequent sessions. As such, he was able to provide a theological basis that helped explain the democratic experience of the American bishops who lived in a pluralistic society in relative peace. Perhaps the United States is the only country where there are great differences in what people believe but where people are not killing one another because of those religious differences.

The topic of religious freedom was dropped from the agenda of the council and only the quick response of some American bishops had it restored. The *Declaration on Religious Freedom* was first conceived of as part of the document on ecumenism, but after much debate it took on a life of its own. Some of the council fathers were fearful of dialogue

with Protestants and even more so with Jews. Discussions of this document were among the most vitriolic of the whole council. Strong feelings and passions surfaced on both sides.

Strong support for the declaration came from most American bishops, and also from Canadian and South American prelates. Bishops from countries behind the Iron Curtain also supported it, not from the perspective of having enjoyed religious liberty but from suffering from the lack of it. On the one hand, some bishops were still suspicious of the effects of the political movements of the nineteenth century that espoused freedom but used violent means in the name of that freedom. On the other, bishops who lived under totalitarian governments that threatened human freedom, especially freedom of religion, realized the need for the church to take a strong stand for freedom.

John XXIII and Cardinal Bea of the Secretariat for Christian Unity also supported a statement on religious freedom. When it appeared that the document may not leave the committee for full discussion by the council fathers, the committee met and invited experts on the issue. These *periti* sat in an outer circle surrounding the committee and could only speak when asked a question. Their answers were to be in Latin. Murray was among those present but so were his adversaries, one of whom made an impassioned plea to remember that "error has no rights." Murray's response is credited with swaying some voting members and moving the issue to the floor of the council.

It may be difficult for us to understand why Murray's teaching was so problematic. We have become somewhat accustomed to the concept of the dignity of the individual person endowed with natural rights and duties and of the duty of the state to protect those human rights. They have been absorbed into the very fiber of our society and our church.

The controversies over this document had more to do with the development of doctrine than with whether freedom of religion was a basic human right. Just one hundred years before, the Syl-

The Church Endorses Religious Freedom

This Vatican Synod declares that the human person has a right to religious freedom. This freedom means that all men are to be immune from coercion on the part of individuals or of social groups and of any human power, in such wise that in matters religious no one is to be forced to act in a manner contrary to his own beliefs. Nor is anyone to be restrained from acting in accordance with his own beliefs, whether privately or publicly, whether alone or in association with others, within due limits.

The Synod further declares that the right to religious freedom has its foundation in the very dignity of the human person, as this dignity is known through the revealed Word of God and by reason itself. The right of the human person to religious freedom is to be recognized in the constitutional law whereby society is governed. Thus it is to become a civil right.

Vatican II, *Declaration on Religious Freedom*

Elizabeth Anne Seton

Mother Seton, known in her youth as "Wild Betty" because of her strong personality, is the first native-born American canonized saint. She was wife, mother, widow, convert, and founder. After the death of her husband in 1805, she converted and moved to Baltimore to support her five children by teaching. In time, she founded the Sisters of Charity and adopted the rule of St. Vincent de Paul.

She and her sisters opened the first free parochial school in Emmitsburg, Maryland. From there, the first sisters traveled to New York and Philadelphia to conduct orphanages. Their work spread to hospitals, clinics, and social welfare centers.

Elizabeth Seton, First American Saint
University of Notre Dame Archives

labus of Errors had condemned "progress, liberalism and modern civilization" and maintained that Catholic doctrine was not open to development. The *Declaration on Religious Freedom* (*Dignitatis Humanae*) officially endorses the development of doctrine — a most significant development for the church.

Dignitatis Humanae teaches that religious freedom is a right founded in the dignity of each individual person. No one is to be forced to act contrary to her or his beliefs nor restrained from acting according to those beliefs. Religious bodies also have rights: freedom to govern themselves, to worship the Supreme Being publicly, to select and train ministers, communicate with religious authorities and communities, erect buildings, and acquire necessary funds.

Education

One of the most creative contributions of American Catholics is its network of schools, academies, and colleges. While religiously sponsored schools do exist in other countries, there is nothing quite like the Catholic educational enterprise as it exists here. Unlike schools in Europe, Canada, and some countries in Latin America, Catholic schools do not receive any government assistance but are supported by the sacrifices of Catholic parents.

Some refer to a Catholic school system, but that would be imposing a structure that does not maintain. There is not one system but rather a collection of different styles of schools that are administered and supported in a variety of ways. Catholic schools may be sponsored by individual parishes, dioceses, religious congregations, and in a few cases by groups of lay persons. There are academies and parish, regional, and diocesan schools. But even that description is too simple.

The family is and was the primary educator, especially the primary religious educator. When Catholics were in the minority with few clergy to serve the life of the community, all education took place in the home. In fact, Bishop John Carroll addressed the need for religious education in the home in one of his first pastoral letters. But as numbers grew, the need for schools became apparent.

This concern for more formal Catholic education is evident in the establishment of schools and universities from our earliest days. Some of the first schools of any kind were established by Catholics. In places as far-flung as Baltimore, North Dakota, California, and Louisiana we read of one-room school houses that flourished under Catholic aegis.

In the nineteenth century, the ideal that every child had the right to a free education and that the state had the duty to provide that education existed in other countries, but none took it on with such fervor as the United States. While not officially supporting one religion or another, state funds subsidized the reading of the Protestant Bible with the Protestant version of the Lord's Prayer recited each day and the Ten Commandments displayed in prominent view. In some areas, especially where other educational facilities did not exist, Catholic schools received state funding.

During the period of great immigration, some Catholics, still in the minority and stinging from anti-Catholic attacks, opened their own schools wherever they could — in rectories, church basements, or one-room cabins. These beginnings were difficult, funds were low, books were scarce and many teachers unprepared. But Catholics had found a way to add the Catechism to "reading, writing and arithmetic." Their love for the faith and their loyalty to the church prompted great sacrifices from poor immigrants.

Some religious congregations opened academies to educate the children of wealthy families, and with the profits that were realized, they conducted free schools for poor children. The education of the poor has, from the beginning, been a high priority. Ursuline sisters founded a free school attached to St. Angela Academy in 1727, before the establishment of the new republic.

The First and Second Plenary Councils of Baltimore urged the establishment of schools. The Third Council in 1884 mandated the building of a

Catholic Schools

Two objects, therefore, dear brethren, we have in view, to multiply our schools, and to perfect them. We must multiply them, till every Catholic child in the land shall have within his reach the means of education. . . . No parish is complete till it has schools adequate to the needs of its children, and the pastor and people of such a parish should feel they have not accomplished their entire duty until the want is supplied.

But then, we must also perfect our schools. We repudiate the idea that the Catholic school need be in any respect inferior to any other school whatsoever. And if hitherto, in some places, our people have acted on the principle that it is better to have an imperfect Catholic school than to have none, let them now push their praiseworthy ambitions still further, and not relax till their schools are elevated to the highest educational excellence. And we implore parents not to hasten to take their children from school, but to give them all the time and all the advantages that they have the capacity to profit by, so that, in after life, their children may "rise up and call them blessed."

Third Plenary Council of Baltimore, 1884

school in every parish where one did not yet exist. Some of the most zealous for the cause suggested that pastors who did not obey should be removed from office and communities that did not support the schools should be placed under interdict. Interdiction means that individual persons or communities may be denied the sacraments and Christian burial. Fortunately, cooler heads prevailed and compromises were made. Even these compromises needed to be toned down by the Vatican.

In many parishes, schools were built before churches. But not all ethnic groups responded to the call for a parish school. Irish, German, Polish, and French immigrants strongly supported the idea but Italians and Mexicans did not. By 1920, only 35 percent of parishes conducted schools, but by 1959, about 59 percent did. Enrollment peaked in the 1960s.

As the number of schools increased in the late nineteenth century, the need for more organization led to the establishment of diocesan and regional offices of education. The Catholic Educational Association was founded in 1904 to improve the character and quality of Catholic education. In our day, the NCEA continues its commitment to support all levels of education but has also turned its attention to the education of Hispanic Americans, global education, the education of the poor, and adult education.

Problems between School and State
The cherished constitutional protection against the establishment of a state religion and the right of Americans to practice their religion has, over the years, come into conflict with the right of parents to educate their children as they see fit. A case in Oregon set the stage for a critical Supreme Court decision. Oregon had, in 1922, passed a law requiring all students to attend public school. Catholics were dismayed at the prospect of closing their schools and brought the case to court. It was fought all the way to the Supreme Court and with the help of other Christian denominations, the ACLU, and John Dewey, the Court unanimously decided against the state.

This did not settle the relationship between Catholic schools and the state. New Jersey provided bus fares for all school children, including

Freedom to Choose

"The fundamental theory of liberty upon which all governments in this Union repose excludes any power of the state to standardize its children by forcing them to accept instruction from public teachers only. The child is not the mere creature of the state. Those who nurture him and direct his destiny have the right coupled with the high duty to recognize and prepare him for additional obligations."[3]

Supreme Court of the United States
June 21, 1925

children in Catholic schools. In that case, the court decided that that practice was not legal since the Constitution forbade the state aiding one or all religions or preferring one religion over the other.

Some communities discovered creative ways to keep the law and at the same time provide Catholic education for their children. In rural areas where German Catholics had already built schools, they leased them to the school district from nine to three. That left the hours before and after "public school hours" for the teaching of religion. The same teachers who taught religion could be hired to teach during the regular school day.

One community in Kansas went a step further. The school board rented the Catholic high school from nine to three and united it with the public high school. The two buildings, in effect, became one town school. Children could take advantage of courses in either building and religion could be taught outside regular hours. The people of the town did not want the arrangement advertised lest outsiders challenge their system.

Religious Education in the Parish

The Confraternity of Christian Doctrine, or the CCD as it is popularly known, is responsible for the religious education of all Catholic children who do not attend Catholic schools. Pius X encouraged the establishment of the CCD in every parish in 1905. In some states, "released time" became the normal way the CCD operated. Catholic school children were dismissed an hour early and children who attended public school came to the Catholic school for religious instruction and preparation for the sacraments. Usually the instruction was conducted by the faculty of the Catholic school.

Pedagogically, the system met many obstacles. Children came to a place that was foreign to them, to be taught by teachers who did not really know them at the end of a school day when energy lagged. They often identified themselves as "publics." In spite of those hurdles, thousands of children learned the foundational teachings of their church.

To facilitate the process the national CCD office arranged for the publication of special texts and teacher's manuals geared to the needs of this apostolate. But CCD never received the support that the parish school did.

As more and more parish schools closed, and in the wake of the changes of Vatican II, pastors and parents began to pay more attention to the religious education of all the children of the parish. Diocesan and parish Offices of Religious Education devised alternative methods for the education of children. The ministry of the DRE (Director of Religious Education) joined the other new ministries on parish staffs.

In most places, professional staff members are responsible for working with and training lay volunteers who work directly with the children. Programs go beyond the released time classes or Sunday School of a previous age and include such things as summer Bible schools, workshops, parent classes, and camps. More recently the religious training of high school students in many parishes has been entrusted to Youth Ministers.

A 1994 study conducted by the Educational Testing Service of Princeton, N.J. found that there was no significant difference between the basic understanding of church doctrine in children who attend Catholic schools and those who attend parish based religious education programs. Previously, about 50 percent of Catholic children attended Catholic schools; that number now is below 20 percent. The vast majority of children receive their religious training in parish programs.

Catechisms

Pre–Vatican II Catholics and some Post–Vatican II Catholics remember well the answers they memorized in the Baltimore Catechism. The catechism was not only the textbook used for the study of religion; it was also the syllabus that determined the course of study.

The discovery of the printing press in the sixteenth century made the catechism a popular tool for spreading the Christian message. Martin Luther is responsible for popularizing the catechism form of questions and answers.

The Council of Trent ordered the publication of a catechism to spread the Catholic teachings to combat the influence of the Protestant catechisms. Catechisms proliferated. Their pattern varied according to the mind of the various authors. Some began with the Ten Commandments, others with the Creed. St. Robert Bellarmine used Augustine's pattern of Faith, Hope, and Love for his work. A common characteristic is that they were all counter-Reformation in spirit.

In spite of the catechisms available from Europe, the bishops of the Third Plenary Council of Baltimore realized the need for a catechism that could be used universally in the United States. This catechism was published first in 1885 and was memorized by children in Catholic schools for more than the next seventy-five years.

After Vatican II, the catechetical formula of question and answer gave way to texts that employed modern educational theory to express the theological understandings of the Second Vatican Council.

In an effort to regularize the teaching of Catholic doctrine around the world, in 1992 the Vatican published a Catechism of the Catholic Church that has come to be called the Universal Catechism. The catechism is meant to present the doctrine of the Catholic Church in a way that is both biblical and liturgical and that takes into consideration the lives of today's Christians. The catechism is meant to be an aid in the transmission of the faith. It does not replace Scripture or the celebration of the liturgy as the primary means of fostering Christian life.

This Universal Catechism is not meant to be used as a text in schools or adult education programs. It is, rather, a resource to be used by publishers of local catechisms and religious educators as they prepare programs for children and adults.

Individual bishops and national conferences of bishops are encouraged to use it to produce local catechisms that "take account of different situations and structures." Indeed, the prologue to the catechism insists that "adapted expositions and catechetical methods required by differences of culture, age, spiritual maturity, and social and ecclesial situations" are the responsibility of the local church and cannot be expected of this catechism.

Although called "universal," the catechism has been criticized as being overly influenced by European theology without taking into consideration theologies from other continents. The English language translation has been criticized for its use of gender-exclusive language. The publication of this English edition was delayed a year to eliminate even more inclusive language.

Higher Education

More than half of all the students enrolled in Catholic schools of higher education worldwide are in the United States. Nowhere in the world are so many lay people studying theology as in this country.

Catholic higher education in this country had a simple beginning. Classes began in Georgetown College (now University) in 1791, the same year as St. Mary's Seminary in Baltimore and the year that the national government began its work. It was not until about fifty years later that other Catholic colleges opened their doors. Holy Cross, Manhattan College, Boston College, and Notre Dame all came into being within a few years of one another. Women's colleges followed suit a few decades later. Among the first were St. Mary's, Indiana, and Trinity College, Washington, D.C.

Maintaining the delicate balance between academic freedom and loyalty to the Catholic Church is crucial for any institution to claim to be both Catholic and an institution of higher learning. Canon 812 in the Code of Canon Law requires that "those who teach theological disciplines in any institution of higher studies must have a mandate from the competent ecclesiastical authority."

State and federal grants and loans ease the burden of higher tuitions but it is still the pattern that Catholic education lays a double burden on citizens. And as in the past, Catholic parents and students are willing to sacrifice for the benefits of such an education. If there were any perceived interference from external religious authorities, state funding could be denied. This could spell the end of Catholic higher education in the United States.

But it is not simply a financial question. Catholic universities have been described as the places where the church does its thinking. Scholars must be free to research and publish their work to be criticized by their peers. It is not the role of theologians only to defend past articulations of doctrine, but also to express the doctrines in a way that is intelligible to people today.

Firm commitment to being Catholic and not going the way of some Ivy League schools that began as religious institutions is obvious in recent statements issued by so many Catholic colleges.

Intellectual Life and Catholicism

When our zeal for intellectual excellence shall have raised up men who will take their place among the first writers and thinkers of their day their very presence will become the most persuasive of arguments to teach the world that no best gift is at war with the spirit of Catholic faith.

–Bishop John Lancaster Spalding at the Third Plenary Council of Baltimore

At the same time, the words of Catholic college presidents in 1967 still hold. ". . . institutional autonomy and academic freedom are essential conditions for life and growth and indeed survival for Catholic universities, as for all universities."[4]

Some Criticism of Catholic Schools

It has long been a criticism of Catholic schools that they do not raise up critical thinkers. The schools were established to protect children from the effects of Protestant teaching; this was accomplished by instilling Catholic truths in catechism form. Memorization rather than understanding was often the norm. Emphasis on obedience, discipline and authority, it is claimed, do not make for inquiring minds. That was probably more true in the past, when Catholics in general claimed more of a certitude about truth and wanted to pass that truth on to the next generation. Unchanging truths, free from ambiguity, were transmitted with confidence. We live with more questions today, and that is reflected in Catholic classrooms.

Another valid criticism of some Catholic schools was that teachers were not always well prepared. Often the need for teachers was so extreme that young members of religious orders were sent to teach before they had training or accreditation. Large classes added to the problem. Some religious congregations did manage to ignore bishops' pleas for sisters and brothers until they had teaching degrees, but many did not.

Critics sometimes assert that Catholic education does not make for good citizens. Recent surveys indicate otherwise. Graduates of Catholic colleges show less anti-Semitism and are more involved in justice issues than Catholics who graduated from public colleges. An issue that is not often referred to is the effect of members of religious congregations on the spiritual life of Catholics. While in no way demeaning their contributions, it must be said that the culture that permeated Catholic schools was that of the convent and monastery. Generations of Catholic children claimed with assurance that they were right because "Sister said…" or "Father said…" Emphasis on rules and religious practices mirrored those of religious life. Lay spirituality did not flourish in such an environment.

Other Educational Agencies

Education cannot be limited to schooling. Magazines, books, newspapers, discussion groups, radio, and television all contribute to the educational endeavor, as do retreats, pilgrimages, and homilies. The Catholic Church may not have *a* religious education program, but it educates in the myriad ways it carries out its mission.

Attempts at a national newspaper were made in the 1820s with the publication of *United States Catholic Miscellany* and *Truth Teller*. Both papers presented a wide range of religious news from this continent and Europe. Other local, diocesan, and ethnic newspapers opened local communities to events beyond their parish or diocese. Today, there is hardly a diocese that does not publish its own paper.

It would be a mistake to think that all Catholic publications are similar to one another. We have only to look at issues of weekly newspapers like *The National Catholic Reporter, Our Sunday Visitor,* and *The Wanderer* to understand the broad spectrum of views that come under the label "Catholic." The same may be said, of course, about the many magazines that claim the title "Catholic."

Some dioceses have invested in telecommunication networks, but on the whole, the church has yet to take full advantage of radio or television.

Conclusion

If you were to conduct a survey about what it means to be Catholic, you would get a variety of answers: it means obeying the pope; it means having to go to Mass on Sunday; it means loving one's neighbor; it means being involved in social justice concerns; it means… Of course, all of the responses have a kernel of truth but none of them is the whole answer.

We would have to add that it means treasuring our tradition. But treasuring tradition does not mean burying the gift that God has given. Like the servants in Matthew's Gospel who are entrusted with riches, we are expected to increase those riches, not bury them. The servants who invested and who increased the treasure are rewarded, but the one who buried it and left it the same as it was received was punished.

The *Dogmatic Constitution on Divine Revelation* asserts, "This tradition which comes from the apostles develops in the Church with the help of the Holy Spirit. For there is a growth in the understanding of the realities and the words which have been handed down." All Christians, not just the clergy, are responsible for that growth in understanding.

The treasure that is tradition is not a static and unchanging reality. It is alive, throbbing, dynamic. We are entrusted with the job to make it flourish. We are a people who are traditioning and that means that we are responsible not only for preserving the tradition but also for contributing to it.

In this chapter, we have discussed ways in which our forebears have contributed to the ongoing mission of the church. Their American experience was gift to the church; they blessed even as they were blessed.

When we say that we are the church, we are implicitly acknowledging that the church is different because of us. Our forebears gave us the example of what it means to be church in such a way that enriches the tradition.

Notes

1. Sally Fitzgerald, ed., *Letters of Flannery O'Connor* (New York: Farrar, Straus and Giroux, 1979), 145.
2. Robert L. Tuzik, *How Firm a Foundation: Leaders of the Liturgical Movement* (Chicago: Liturgical Training Publications, 1990), 154.
3. Quoted in John Tracy Ellis, ed., *Documents of American Catholic History* (Milwaukee: Bruce Publishing Co., 1956), 638.
4. Quoted in William Barnaby Flaherty, *American Catholic Heritage* (Kansas City: Sheed and Ward, 1991) 96.

4

The Challenge of Vatican II

The Man Who Called the Council

Pope John XXIII was elected as an interim pope when the College of Cardinals could not agree on a younger man. He was an old man when elected and the cardinals thought that his reign would be short and uneventful. In a few years, they figured, they would be back to elect another pope and by that time there may be a chance for agreement.

Anecdotes about this cheerful, friendly pope filled the secular press. On one occasion, he practiced over and over what to call the First Lady when she visited Rome. "Madame, Madame Kennedy, Mrs. Kennedy, Ma-

Pope John XXIII
University of Notre Dame Archives

dame…" When she entered the room, he opened his arms and exclaimed, "Jacqueline."

His informality delighted the world after the staid Pius XII. It also led some to think of him as a simple pastor and to forget his political background.

John was from peasant stock but had served as seminary professor, president of the Italian branch of the Society for the Propagation of the Faith, Apostolic Visitor to Sofia, Apostolic Delegate to Istanbul, Apostolic Nuncio to post-war France, and finally Patriarch of Venice. His experience of church was more colorful than most.

He raised the salaries of Vatican employees and suggested that the men who had to carry him on the *sedes*

Bishops at the Second Vatican Council
University of Notre Dame Archives

gestoria (papal chair used at that time for public audiences) be given more money since he weighed so much more than Pius XII, his predecessor.

John called the council to address the "signs of the times," an expression previously used to indicate the dire events preceding the end of the world. John's more optimistic use refers to historic events in which we may recognize the revelation of God. He spoke of *aggiornamento*, bringing the church up to date; of opening the windows to let fresh air in; of bringing the bishops of the world together so that they may educate one another to the sufferings of the world. His optimism about the human condition was not shared by all and he chided "the prophets of gloom, who are always forecasting disaster, as if the end of the world were at hand."

The Second Vatican Council

The twenty-first Ecumenical Council met from 1961 to 1965 and was like no council before it. The most easily recognized difference was the presence of native bishops from Africa, Asia, and Latin America. There were more than two thousand participants, three times as many participants as at Vatican I (1869–1870) and more than twenty times the number at the Council of Trent (1545–1563).

The invention of the printing press gave wider airing of Trent's proclamations than earlier councils had received but relatively few persons could read and transportation was slow. It is generally thought that most Catholics did not even know there was a council in session and that the effects took at least a century to take hold.

At the time of Vatican I communications were better but could not compare with the almost instantaneous reports from Vatican II that television and radio brought to homes around the world. The presence of the media altered past patterns of communication.

American Bishops at the Council

While the American bishops at the First Vatican Council made their presence felt, especially in the discussion on infallibility, American bishops at the next council had a more significant effect. At Vatican I only one American served on a preparatory committee. Vatican II saw forty-three in that capacity. More than sixty expert theologians advised the bishops.

Though they may have disagreed on different issues, New York's conservative Cardinal Francis Spellman and Chicago's liberal Cardinal Meyer assumed leadership roles in various committee meetings. Along with Cardinals Richard Cushing of Boston, Shehan of Baltimore, and Ritter of St. Louis they were primarily responsible for the church's statement that Jews were not responsible for the death of Christ. Their American theological advisors provided strong enough theological support for claiming that Jews had not lost divine favor and that God is still faithful to the Chosen People.

As a result, the section on Jews in the *Declaration on the Relationship of the Church to Non-Christian Religions* was accepted in spite of some resistance from other bishops. Bishops from predominantly Moslem lands feared that any statement in support of Jews would be interpreted politically and have negative repercussions on Christians. But the sensitivity of European and American bishops to the Holocaust, plus the religious experience of the Americans in a pluralistic society, made some statement necessary.

The World Council of Churches had already issued a statement on anti-Semitism in 1961 in New Delhi. Neither the Protestant nor the Catholic statement acknowledges guilt on the part of the church for fostering prejudice against Jews through the ages. The Vatican document, while appreciated by many Jews as a first step in the process of reconciliation, has also been criticized as "a unilateral pronouncement by one party which presumes to redress on its own terms a wrong which it does not admit."[1]

Some of the powerful American hierarchy did not play a significant role at the council. Cardinal Richard Cushing of Boston is said to have admitted that he returned to Boston rather than stay in Rome because he couldn't understand the Latin used at the council sessions, and even if he could, he would have been put to sleep. Even the powerful Spellman played a less significant role than might have been expected. Known as a close friend of Pius XII and of President Franklin D. Roosevelt, military chaplain who visited almost all the World War II battlefields, proponent of movie censorship, and outspoken anti-Communist, Spellman was one of the most influential American churchmen before the council. But he also had a reputation for his opposition to lay involvement, liturgical renewal, ecumenism, and so-called "liberal Catholicism." To his credit, he adjusted to the changes with equanimity if not enthusiasm.

The documents on ecumenism and the church's relationship to non-Christian religions were of vital interest to American bishops, living as they did in a more pluralistic society than many other bishops. We have already alluded to the importance of the decree on religious freedom in chapter two. At Vatican II "Americanism" came to be seen in a more positive light rather than as an evil attacking the life of the church.

The Third Epoch of the Church

The great theologian Karl Rahner described the effects of Vatican II as the coming of the Third Church. He divided the past twenty centuries of the church's life into three epochs: Jewish Christianity, Hellenic-Western Christianity, and the World Church that is now in the process of development. History is not so neatly divided into periods, of course, and there have been major developments in other historical periods. The post-Reformation church is different from the medieval church and they are both different from the early church. But the radical theological break that we are witnessing, according to Rahner, occurred only once before.

When Paul argued that circumcision was no longer necessary for followers of Jesus, the break with Jewish Christianity was something that Jesus had never envisioned. Jesus was about the revitalization of Judaism, not the establishment of a new religion. The church was established by the disciples who were all Jews until Paul opened the gates wide for non-Jews to enter, and a radically new creation came into being. Transferring the Sabbath from Saturday to Sunday in memory of the day that Jesus rose from the dead and moving the center from Jerusalem to Rome are indications of the striking break that was effected.

The move toward becoming a world church is causing and will continue to cause transformations that we have yet fully to realize. Before the council, Christianity was shipped, somewhat like a product, from Europe and North America to the rest of the world to be accepted and consumed in the form in which it was received. There was no expecta-tion that the sender would be required to change.

But the council, in opening, as it did, to the non-Western world, inaugurated a transformation that is on a par with Paul's. No longer is it possible for the Roman church to remain unchanged by the history, customs, liturgical practices, and lifestyles of Africans, Asians, and Latin Americans.

Questions arise, such as whether or not it is necessary or even appropriate for grape wine to be used in areas where grapes are not native to the area; whether patriarchs in Africa may, like Abraham, keep more than one wife; whether a celibate priesthood is appropriate in all areas. These questions focus on facets of traditional Christianity that are of low theological priority. No one is questioning whether the Trinity or the true divinity and humanity of Jesus or the efficacy of the sacramental system ought to be rethought. What is being questioned is whether or not Romanized customs and practices are necessary for all Catholics.

The bishops gathered for the council did not foresee this Third Church, but in redefining the church as the Church *in* the Modern World they paved the way for it.

Gustavo Gutiérrez, the father of liberation the-

Vatican II: Just the Beginning

[Vatican II's] inadequacy was due partly to its lack of an adequate social analysis of what was going on in the world at the time. It had no real sense of the struggles of the poor, the working class, of women, of oppressed racial groups. It did not deal seriously with racism and white supremacy, with sexism and male dominance, with classism and capitalist exploitation. It did not come to terms with the Russian Revolution or even consider seriously the Chinese and Cuban revolutions and the Vietnamese struggle. There was no deep dialogue with other religions, cultures, and ideologies as offering alternative analyses and worldviews to the white Western, capitalist, male mind-set that still dominated Catholicism... The Council had no clear vision of the type of world it envisioned as against the present exploitative world system with its assault on nature by the exhaustion of non-renewable resources and environmental pollution. Hence it did not propose relevant practical goals in the real world and strategies for transforming mentalities and structures.[2]

–Tissa Balasuriya, Sri Lankan Theologian

ology, has maintained that Vatican II was just what it said, a council for and about the church in the modern world, not the church in the developing world. While native bishops from Asia, Africa, and Latin America attended, the dominant influence was from Europe and North America. The questions faced by the church on other continents is a development that has occurred since the council. The critique of theologians from the Third World reminds us not to romanticize the council, even as we rejoice in its accomplishments. We may be in the infancy of a world church, but we have not yet attained being truly "Catholic."

The Documents Promulgated at Vatican II

The Vatican II documents concerning the role of the church differ from previous writings of the church in that they are more biblically and theologically grounded. Earlier documents depended more on natural law and scholastic philosophy. The complexities of modern life, technological advances, and competing philosophies worked together to challenge the church to search its basic beliefs and to devise an ecclesiology less dependent on rational thought and more on Christian faith.

Not every statement proclaimed by councils carries the same weight. Sometimes the title gives us a clue about the significance of a particular document. Constitutions deal with those things that constitute the essence of the church. As such, they are more authoritative than decrees and declarations which deal with pastoral and practical issues. Vatican II issued sixteen documents, of which two are constitutions on the church itself: the *Dogmatic Constitution on the Church* and the *Pastoral Constitution on the Church in the Modern World*.

The official designation of the various documents is not the only determinant as to their significance. The reception by the Catholic community also determines the effect that they will have on the life of the church. Perhaps the most obvious example of this is the document on liturgy that we have already discussed. In spite of the difficulties some Catholics experienced, the changes that have been effected in the church's liturgical life are a sign of how readily many accepted the proposals. We have already discussed the impact of the *Declaration on Religious Freedom*; although declarations are the least of the three designations, the document has taken on great import.

One last word of introduction before we discuss specific documents produced by the council. The documents as finally agreed on are the result of debate, argument, disagreement, lobbying, negotiations, and compromise. There was not universal agreement on any idea, and sometimes no one was perfectly satisfied with the final statement. But once they were accepted by vote, they became the foundation for the church's life.

Lumen Gentium: *Dogmatic Constitution on the Church*

Bishop Emil de Smidt denounced the first schema of *Lumen Gentium* as "clericalism, juridicism and

Evolution of *Lumen Gentium*

We declare, moreover, that whether one considers its existence or its constitution, the Church of Christ is an everlasting and indefectible society, and that, after it, no more complete or perfect economy of salvation is to be hoped for in this world. . . . It is free and immune from every danger of error and untruth.

First draft presented and rejected

By her relationship with Christ, the Church is a kind of sacrament or sign of intimate union with God and of the unity of all humankind.

Fourth and approved draft

triumphalism." Following the usual pattern, it discussed the hierarchy first and then the laity, thus modelling an institutional ecclesiology.

That schema was entitled "The Nature of the Church Militant." It took four drafts and numerous revisions before the church decided to present itself to the world as Mystery of God rather than as a militant body. The second chapter gave new insights into what it means to be Christian when it referred to all Christians as the People of God.

People of God. The Hebrew scriptures call Israel "the People of God" to distinguish them from other nations, the *goyim*. They had the guarantee, "I will set my dwelling among you. Ever present in your midst, I will be your God and you will be my people" (Lev. 26:11–12).

Early Christians arrogated the title "People of God" for themselves. The author of the First Epistle of Peter assures the new Gentile converts that they are "a chosen race, a royal priesthood, a holy nation, a people [God] claims for his own to proclaim the glorious works of the One who called you out of darkness into his marvelous light." These words echo Yahweh's pledge to the Hebrews in the desert at Sinai. The epistle continues, "Once you were no people, but now you are God's people; once there was no mercy for you, but now you have found mercy" (2:10).

In the centuries before Vatican II, the image of "People of God" was overshadowed by a belief that the church was a divine and perfect institution without error or failure. While it was readily acknowledged that there might be sinners in the church, no one spoke of the church itself as being involved in sin. So, it was a major shift in self-understanding for the church to admit to being God's people, related to God by covenant. It also involves the awareness that the covenant was often broken and while "holding sinners in its embrace, is at the same time holy and always in need of being purified and incessantly pursues the path of penance and renewal"(*Lumen Gentium* [LG], #8).

In case anyone might wonder who is included in the People of God, we are assured, "Everything that has been said so far concerning the People of God applies equally to the laity, religious and clergy"(LG, #30). The church is presented as the People of God whose members have different roles but share the same mission. It is because of the use of the metaphor "People of God" that the faithful now perceive themselves as responsible participants in rather than passive members of the church.

The Roman church does not identify itself as the People of God but holds that all who believe in Christ are the new People of God, an insight of significant ecumenical impact.

Body of Christ. The scriptures offers many images and metaphors for God such as Lord, Rock, Shepherd, Father, Mother, King, Judge. In the same way, the church uses many images to describe itself: the vine tended by the Divine Vinedresser, the Flock of the Good Shepherd, the Temple of God, our Mother, the Spouse of the Lamb. The multiplication of metaphors and images suggests that we are dealing with mystery. Each metaphor provides some insight into the mystery of what the church is, but no metaphor is able to carry the whole meaning by itself.

One of the most significant images besides People of God is Body of Christ, an image central to Paul's thinking but one that did not get much attention in the recent past. All who are baptized are baptized into one Body — one Body with many members. This document moves on from the teaching of Pius XII that the Body of Christ is the same as the Roman Catholic Church. *Mystici Corporis* (1943) stated that the Body of Christ *is* the Roman Catholic Church. *Lumen Gentium* develops that thought and claims that the Body of Christ "subsists in" the Catholic Church, not that it is the same as the Catholic Church. This significant change in language has opened the door for more a ecumenical theological development.

The role of the clergy. This topic will receive fuller attention in chapter five. The chapter on the clergy in *Lumen Gentium* does not use monarchical language in describing the government of the church but holds collegiality as the ideal and model for the relationship among bishops and between the bishops and the pope. Collegiality is the recommended mode for the bishops to interact both locally and internationally, a clear move from a hierarchical model. Bishops are learning to act collegially when they are convened in council or dispersed in their various dioceses throughout the world. In either case, they act in union with the pope and share in the infallibility of the church.

The idea of collegiality was originally presented as the way that bishops would interact, but the benefits of collegiality encouraged many dioceses and parishes to attempt to act collegially and to minister in a collaborate manner. It is not easy for groups to change their mode of relating, but many who have struggled to learn alternative structures and methods consider the results worth the effort.

While the practice of collegiality and collaboration in ministry and decision-making is spreading, too little has been done to develop theology to support these efforts. Parish councils, diocesan boards and committees, priest councils, national conferences of bishops, and synods are not simply political bodies. They are the way the church operates. As such they need a firm theological base for the manner in which they relate to one another and

Lay Ministry

Sharing the Word
Sister of St. Joseph, Brentwood, New York

to the universal church. The lack of that foundation is making the move toward collegiality unnecessarily difficult.

The role of the laity. We will discuss the role of the laity more fully in chapter five but some attention needs to be paid here to a radical change in official language when speaking of the laity. Previously, lay involvement in the church was spoken of as participation in the mission of the hierarchy. *Lumen Gentium* changes only a few words but adds a whole new meaning. It speaks of "participation in the saving mission of the church itself" (LG, #33). The mission of church itself which is the mission of the Christ is the defining character of the laity's responsibility. Christians assume responsibility for the mission of the church by virtue of their baptism and confirmation, not by delegation from bishops or pastors.

Americans answered that challenge with energy and commitment. Young people cannot imagine a church without Eucharistic ministers, lectors, parish councils, or permanent deacons. Lay involvement, while not at the level hoped for, has changed the face of Catholic parishes and dioceses.

It is well to recall that this document was promulgated before the so-called "priest shortage" and therefore was not responding to perceived needs for more people to be involved in ministry. Lay people are not involved in ministry to make up for a lack of priests but because it is their baptismal right and obligation.

The role of the Blessed Virgin Mary, Mother of God, in the mystery of Christ and the church. Originally, a separate document on Mary was planned but as the church redefined itself and its members, it became obvious that the discussion on Mary belonged in the discussion on the church. As disciple par excellence, she is the model for Christians and for the church itself. This was a difficult decision, and in passing by only four votes it was the closest vote of the council.

Those who did not want a separate document on Mary argued that the semi-deification of Mary that occurred among some Catholics did not bring some devotees to Christ. Mary, not Christ, was sometimes the focus of prayer and piety. Her relationship to Christ and to the church is better represented by placing her in the discussion on the church.

Gaudium et Spes: *The Pastoral Constitution on the Church in the Modern World*

Lumen Gentium spoke of the church as People of God and Body of Christ, both of which refer to the church as mystery, as a sacrament of God's presence. *Gaudium et Spes, the Pastoral Constitution on the Church in the Modern World*, seeks to answer a different question, one that Cardinal Suenens suggested the world was asking: "Church of Christ, what do you say of yourself?" It investigates the role of the church vis-à-vis the world. The document is addressed not just to Catholics, or even to Christians, but to all of humanity. "For the Council yearns to explain to everyone how it conceives of the presence and activity of the Church in the world of today" (*Gaudium et Spes* [GS], #2).

Gaudium et Spes talks about the church as it relates to the world. It rejects the notion that religion is a private affair that has nothing to do with conditions in society, and it does this so strongly that it identifies it as one of the "gravest errors of our time" (GS, #43).

This document makes frequent reference to *community*, speaking of the human community in the richness of its being: it is a political community, economic community, social community, a community of nations. Men and women, made in the image of God, are, by their very nature, social beings who develop their potential and their gifts in their relationship with one another. The social nature of human beings "makes it evident that the progress of the human person and the advance of society itself hinge on each other" (GS, #25). We do not become human in a vacuum but only in community; in fact, the development of human beings and of society hang on one another.

Discussion about community is balanced with insistence on individual human dignity. This dignity may be recognized in the development of the human mind, in the search for truth and wisdom, and in the development of a moral conscience. Hu-

---

The Church in the Modern World

They are mistaken who, knowing that we have here no abiding city but seek one which is to come, think that they may therefore shirk their earthly responsibilities. For they are forgetting that by the faith itself they are more than ever obliged to measure up to these duties, each according to his proper vocation.

Nor, on the contrary, are they any less wide of the mark who think that religion consists in acts of worship alone and in the discharge of certain moral obligations, and who imagine they can plunge themselves into earthly affairs in such a way as to imply that these are altogether divorced from the religious life. This split between the faith which many profess and their daily lives deserves to be counted among the more serious errors of our age.

Gaudium et Spes, #43

Human Dignity

Therefore, there must be made available to all men [and women], everything necessary for leading a life truly human, such as food, clothing, and shelter; the right to choose a state of life freely and to found a family, the right to education, to employment, to a good reputation, to respect, to appropriate information, to activity in accord with the upright norm of one's own conscience, to protection of privacy and to rightful freedom in matters religious too.

Gaudium et Spes, #26

man dignity is also evident in authentic freedom, "an exceptional sign of the divine image." Finally, human dignity is evident because humans have been created by God "for a blissful purpose beyond the reach of earthly misery" (GS, #18). But the greatest evidence of human dignity is the call to communion with God (GS, #19). Women and men are valued not because of their nationality or religion, their intelligence or their net worth. Women and men are valued because they come from God and are called to intimate union with God.

While the bishops acknowledge the efforts made by nations toward mutual dependence, they balance that optimistic view with the more sober realization that "we have not seen the last of bitter political, social and economic hostility, and racial and ideological antagonism, nor are we free from the specter of a war of total destruction" (GS, #4).

Urgent problems. *Gaudium et Spes* is divided into two sections. The first focuses on the dignity of the human person, the community of humankind, human activity in the universe and the role of the church in the modern world. The second section attends to the "urgent problems" the bishops rec-

ognized in the world: marriage and the family, human culture, life in its economic, social, and political dimensions, the bonds between the family of nations, and peace.

Regarding marriage, *Gaudium et Spes* moves on from a position that presented procreation as the primary end of marriage and the love of spouses as its secondary end. Conjugal love is described as being important in itself and even as "merging the human with the divine" and leading to the free and mutual gift of the spouses to each other. In fact, "this love is uniquely expressed and perfected through the marital act" (GS, #49). Only after addressing the mutual love of spouses does the document speak of procreation.

This shift in the theology of marriage is perhaps best indicated by the change of language from contract to marriage covenant. As a pledge of faithfulness and shared intimacy, the covenant of marriage speaks less to the legal aspect of marriage than to the mystery of the sacrament. The covenant is a reminder that each sacramental marriage is a sign, a sacrament of the love of God and the love of human beings for each other.

The other urgent problems are addressed elsewhere in this book but a few words seem appropriate here. *Gaudium et Spes* states that the church is not bound to any "particular form of human culture, nor to any political, economic or social system" (GS, #42). At the same time, the church is responsible for attending to the "signs of the times" that are evident in these systems and for interpreting them in the light of the gospel. In this section can be recognized dependence on the social teaching of the church from Leo XIII's *Rerum Novarum* (1891) to John XXIII's *Pacem in Terris* (1963).

Gaudium et Spes provides the foundation for the American bishops' pastoral letter on peace. Both documents state that "peace is not merely the absence of war," but "an enterprise of justice."

Robert McAfee Brown, one of the Protestant observers at the council, fears that the church may be in danger of losing sight of its prophetic edge because the document may be too uncritical of the world. He warns: "The document minimizes the degree to which the gospel is also a scandal and a stumbling-block, by which men [and women] can be offended as well as uplifted...The making of common cause with others must not be achieved at the price of blunting the uniqueness and distinctness of the Christian message."[3]

Reception by the faithful. It would matter hardly at all what the Council said if Catholics around the world ignored the documents. The acceptance and interpretation of ecclesial statements is called "reception" by the theological community. The entire body of the faithful, clergy and laity, is the final judge of how much any particular formulation will affect the church. The sense of the faithful or *sensus fidelium* is the guarantor and protector of doctrine. We might call it "believer's instinct," or the presence of the Holy Spirit, but it is the way that the church lives out the words that have been spoken.

As a result of this sense of the faithful, some statements have greater significance than others. Their acceptance affects the way Catholics at large contribute to the development of doctrine. Having said this, we have to admit that most Catholics have not read the documents or, at best, have only heard some of the council decisions preached and taught. But — and this is an important *but* — "reception" does not follow from a merely intellectual approach but from the symbols, metaphors, rituals, and actions that the documents have spawned. It is liturgical practice, Scripture study groups, ecumenical discussions, and the involvement of the laity in parish and diocesan councils and the like that give life to the council's words.

The acceptance of the principles of Vatican II has been so widespread that most Catholics cannot remember when things were different. It is difficult for young Catholic Americans to imagine a Eucharist at which the priest was turned away from the congregation who were somewhat passive and who did not understand the language, even when the prayers were spoken aloud. It is difficult for them to imagine a time when Scripture was not central to Catholic spirituality. It is difficult for them to imagine a time when the laity did not presume it had the right and duty to be involved in "church affairs." The changes that the Council brought about have become part of who we are; we hardly remember when things were otherwise.

Conscience and Authority

It should come as no surprise that sixteen documents written by different committees over a period of four years have points of disjunction. One of these conflicts occurs between the obligation to follow one's conscience and the obedience demanded to the hierarchy.

Gaudium et Spes describes conscience as the most secret core and sanctuary of human beings, the place where they are alone with God whose voice echoes in their depths. The law inscribed on the human heart by God must be obeyed. It is a voice that ever calls persons to love, to accomplish good and avoid evil. Of course, not all persons develop a good conscience, and sometimes "conscience is by degrees almost blinded through the habit of committing sin" (GS, #16). But the council upholds the supremacy of conscience in spite of that danger.

The laity are warned that they cannot expect the clergy to have an answer to every problem. While they must themselves be guided by Christian wisdom and attend to the teaching authority of the church, they are responsible for cultivating an informed conscience themselves and for following that conscience (GS, #43).

Lumen Gentium, on the other hand insists that the faithful are obliged to submit to the teachings of their bishops in matters of faith and morals and "to adhere to it with a ready and respectful allegiance of mind." This loyal submission is required in a special way to the authority of the pope even when he is not speaking *ex cathedra* ("from the chair," a reference to infallibility) (LG, #25). The tension between the two statements became evident soon after the council in the response of the faithful to the encyclical

The Importance of Conscience

As witnesses to a spirited tradition which accepts enlightened consciences, even when honestly mistaken, as the immediate arbiter of moral decisions, we can only feel reassured by this evidence of individual responsibility and the decline of uncritical conformism to patterns, some of which included strong moral elements to be sure, but also included political, social, cultural, and like controls not necessarily in conformity with the mind and heart of the Church.

1968 Statement of American Bishops in support of conscientious objectors

Humanae Vitae regarding birth control.

The implications of this teaching have also had particular consequences for Catholics opposed to serving in the military. Pope Pius XII taught that conscientious objection was not an appropriate response when a citizen's country was involved in a just war. The teaching on the supremacy of conscience opened the door for American bishops in 1980 to issue a statement "On Registration and Conscription for Miliary Service" supporting conscientious objectors as long as they accepted some other kind of service. They repeated their support in the Pastoral "The Challenge of Peace" three years later.

The *Declaration on Religious Freedom* would not have been possible without a commitment to the preeminence of conscience. Each person must be free to worship God as his or her conscience directs. Given our past history, the implications are staggering.

Tension is evident today in the controversies between some theologians and bishops regarding dissent. Private dissent on the part of competent persons concerning noninfallible teachings may not always have been emphasized, but it is part of Catholic tradition.

American bishops addressed public dissent in their 1968 pastoral letter, "Human Life in Our Day." They taught that theologians may engage in public dissent if the reasons are serious and well-founded and if the teaching authority of the church is not

denounced. Moreover, care must be taken in the manner of dissent so that the less theologically sophisticated will not be scandalized. That stance has been challenged by Archbishop James Hickey and Cardinal Joseph Ratzinger.

There are principles to be considered in making an argument for the inviolability of conscience. First, the teaching of the church must be respected and considered a major resource for moral decision-making. But if, after reflection, study, prayer and consultation there is disagreement, persons who disagree must obey their consciences. Secondly, the fundamental values upheld by the church are not to be repudiated if there is disagreement in a particular case. Thirdly, attention needs to be paid to other resources besides official teachings: Scripture, respected friends and relatives, scientific findings, and elements in culture that bear on the issue. These are not, of course, the final word, but they do need to be attended to in making moral decisions.

American Bishops on Economy and War

There can be no question that the American hierarchy has taken seriously the principles laid down in *Gaudium et Spes*. They have taken to heart its words, "Let them [bishops] prepare themselves by careful study to meet and play their part in dialogue with the world and with men [sic] of all shades of opinion" (GS, #43). They have issued forceful statements and inaugurated programs to deal with the major social problems of our day. Having identified the church as servant to the world, the bishops have individually and corporately confronted poverty, racial and religious prejudice, hunger, housing, violence in the streets, sexual abuse, the environment, and other social issues from the perspective of the gospel.

The impact of the council, especially *Gaudium et Spes*, on the thinking of the American hierarchy is evident in the pastoral letters "The Challenge of Peace: God's Promise and Our Response" and "Economic Justice for All: Catholic Social Teaching and the U.S. Economy." It is even evident in the process used in the writing of these documents. The National Conference of Catholic Bishops solicited widespread consultation from experts and concerned persons; they engaged the media in each step of the operation. The secrecy of earlier ages was eliminated as an American spirit of openness made bishops learners as well as teachers.

"The Challenge of Peace" (1983) raised questions about the morality of the use of nuclear arms as well as the possibility of a just war in these modern times. The bishops call for a policy of "no first use" of nuclear weapons on the part of the United States. Drawing on the just war theory and nonviolent traditions of the church, the document addresses the policy of deterrence, arms control, and the promotion of peace.

The bishops do not condemn nuclear war but they are skeptical about its moral acceptability. They question the acceptance of nuclear weapons as a deterrent to war because of the danger of escalating the arms race and the cost to the poor as a result of military spending. In giving "a strictly conditioned moral acceptance" of nuclear deterrence, the bishops firmly state that it is never morally acceptable when it kills innocent people. They call for a bilateral and verifiable halt to new systems, cuts in the stockpiles of superpowers, and a comprehensive test-ban treaty.

Peace, they recall from *Gaudium et Spes*, is not an absence of war but the presence of justice.

In "Economic Justice for All" (1986) the bishops hold governments responsible for protecting the rights of all citizens, but especially the poor. In fact, the way that public policies protect the poor is the litmus test of how just that society is. Unemployment, especially among minorities, is declared intolerable; governments should give priority to the creation of jobs that provide adequate pay and decent working conditions. Changes in social and economic structures that would empower the poor and enable them to help themselves are required.

While holding governments responsible for creating a society that secures basic justice for all its members, the bishops boldly state that "all the moral principles that govern the just operation of any economic endeavor apply to the Church and its agencies and institutions; indeed the Church should be exemplary." The church must be just in its economic practices by paying just wages, respecting rights of employees, and being responsible about investments and property.

Like the documents they draw upon, these texts were not warmly received by all segments of society. Some critics saw the bishops as interfering in politics instead of concerning themselves about religious affairs. But the bishops addressed social issues because they perceived them as part of their religious mission. The bishops were both vilified and congratulated as Catholics and others debated the merits of their words. What could not be debated was the fact that the Catholic Church had taken strong stands on substantive issues and had generated significant discussions in the public forum, even if they have not had the hoped-for impact on national policy.

The closing remarks of *Gaudium et Spes* provide a model for theological discussions as well as for daily living: "Let there be unity in what is necessary, freedom in what is unsettled and charity in any case" (GS, # 92).

Notes

1. Claude Nelson, *A Response to the Declaration on the Relationship of the Church to Non-Christian Religions* in *The Documents of Vatican II*, Walter M. Abbott, S.J. (New York: America Press, 1966), 669–670.
2. Tissa Balasuriya, *Planetary Theology*, (Maryknoll N.Y.: Orbis Books, 1984), 148.
3. Robert McAfee Brown, *Response to Pastoral Constitution on the Church in the Modern World* in *The Documents of Vatican II*, Walter M. Abbott, S.J., 669–70.

5
Ministry in All Its Diversity

Toward a Wider Definition of Ministry

I f you were to look up the word *minister* in the index of *The Documents of Vatican II* published immediately after the Council, you will find the entry "see Clergy, Priests." There seems to have been fewer questions about the concept of ministry and more agreement about its meaning than today. The word did not carry the ambiguities that have developed in the past few decades. Ministry has taken on a variety of meanings, partly as a result of the variety of descriptions that the church proposed for itself at Vatican II.

In the recent past, ministry referred to the service performed by the ordained clergy; the word was not used to describe what members of religious congregations did. The work of sisters and brothers in religious congregations was called the apostolate. Laity were the people who were the objects of ministry and the apostolate.

Why the shift in understanding? The easy answer, of course is that the Second Vatican Council mandated some changes. But that is too easy and

Sharing Table Ministry
Notre Dame Magazine

only part of the story. The council was responding to changes in society, trying to open the windows of the church to the twentieth century. The council fathers were critically aware of the contemporary developments that made the church appear out of touch with the realities of people's lives.

John XXIII spoke of the "signs of the times" when he referred to developments in society that demanded special attention from the church. More than three decades ago, Pope John recognized the rise of the working class in economic and social affairs, the women's movement, and the proliferation of newly independent nations as crucial issues facing the church and society. Each of the signs has to do with individuals and people of a particular country or class redefining themselves. Each, in turn, has had a profound effect on the workings of the church, both locally and universally.

But Pope John's signs are only part of the story. When we try to list events that have affected the way the church identifies itself, such things as the Industrial Revolution, the Enlightenment, and advances in knowledge, especially scientific knowledge need to be taken into consideration.

The word *ministry* has expanded so that it is difficult to agree about its meaning. Even the National Council of Catholic Bishops is not in agreement as to the exact meaning. A few years ago, the administrative board decided that the word ministry would refer to activities of bishops, priests, and deacons or lay persons commissioned by the church. All other works would be called Christian service.

The theologians among the bishops thought it premature to close off the discussion of the meaning of the word. They,

Ministry is reaching out to others.
Notre Dame Magazine

like we, are still in the process of defining what the word shall mean in our day.

Some definitions of ministry are quite narrow, maintaining that ministry is the work of the hierarchy; others are very broad identifying every good work as ministry. Perhaps the answer lies somewhere in the middle.

Distinguishing Marks of Ministry

As I see it, ministry has at least four distinguishing marks:

1. It is specific service to the needs of persons, communities, or systems,
2. carried out in the name of Christ,
3. arising from and rooted in the church and
4. contributing to the coming of the Reign of God.

Regarding the first point: Ministry is specific service to the needs of persons, communities, or systems. If there were no suffering, no brokenness, no division, no sin in the world, we would not need ministers. We are called to ministry in order to heal, redeem, and liberate humanity and all of creation from evil and sin. Ministry is one response to suffering in the world. The first mark, therefore, is that our action is in answer to a need or deprivation experienced by persons and institutions.

Ministry is the name we give to service done because of our relationship with Christ. When we act in our own name, the work we do may be graced but it is not ministry. We often perform generous service to friends, family, and neighbors out of our concern for them. We

Baptism Calls Us to Ministry
Sisters of St. Joseph, Brentwood, NY

This may be a good time to emphasize that ministry is not better than, more noble than, or more graced than other good works. Indeed, the unselfish and often extravagantly charitable service carried out by Jews, Muslims, and others witnesses to this.

Some theologians speak of the spontaneous responses to suffering that face us every day as "general ministries." Actions such as visiting the sick, consoling those who mourn, and giving food and drink to hungry persons or donating money to a worthy cause might be included. In not referring to these works as ministry, I am not denigrating them but emphasizing that they are in themselves wonderful and graced. We do not have to label everything ministry to consider it graced, grace-full, pleasing to God, and beneficial to the church and the world.

My third point, that ministry arises from and is rooted in the church, arises from the conviction that the mission and ministry of the church is the

Body of Christ
Sisters of St. Joseph, Brentwood, New York

visit Grandma on her birthday (and more often, it is hoped); we help a friend paint his house; we collect money for the local public television station. All are good in themselves but I would not label them ministry since they are not intentionally carried out in the name of the Risen Christ. I do not, therefore, include every good work, every kind deed, every act of "Christian charity" under the rubric of ministry.

In the same way, I do not include prayer in the definition of ministry. While prayer may be a response to suffering and sin, it does not constitute service. Perhaps excluding prayer from the definition of ministry makes it easier to understand that exclusion from the label *ministry* is not a negative judgment. It may be that in trying to include every good work under ministry, we are implicitly admitting that we believe that there is an automatic hierarchy of sorts that places ministry higher than other acts of charity and justice.

Earthly Progress and the Reign of God

Earthly progress must be carefully distinguished from the growth of Christ's kingdom. Nevertheless, to the extent that the former can contribute to the better ordering of human society, it is of vital concern to the kingdom of God.

For after we have obeyed the Lord, and in His Spirit nurtured on earth the values of human dignity, brotherhood and freedom, and indeed all the good fruits of our nature and enterprise, we will find them again, but freed of stain, burnished and transfigured. This will be so when Christ hands over to the Father a kingdom eternal and universal: "a kingdom of truth and life, of holiness and grace, of justice, love and peace" [Preface for the Feast of Christ the King]. On this earth, that kingdom is already present in mystery. When the Lord returns, it will be brought into full flower.

Gaudium et Spes, #39

Lay Leadership Graduates
Catholic News Service

mission and ministry of each Christian. The question here is what is meant by the church.

If we were to assume that the hierarchy is the church, then all ministries would of necessity belong to and depend on the hierarchy. The suggestion of the National Conference of Catholic Bishops that only the service of the ordained or those commissioned by a bishop or pastor is ministry springs from that understanding of church.

But the church *community* may also send forth ministers. Catholic Worker Houses, shelters for battered women sponsored by many religious congregations, young college graduates who volunteer in schools and clinics are extraordinary examples of non-ecclesiastically sponsored ministries that arise out of the church community. Rooting ministry in the church, whether perceived primarily as institution or as community, is an attempt to avoid "Lone Ranger" ministries.

Ministry may be either internal, concerned with the life of the church, or external, concerned with the church's mission to the world. In either case, it is sharing in the mission of the church. The internal ministries are necessary so that the church may carry out its external ministries. The church does not exist for itself but for the sake of the world.

My fourth point is that ministry contributes to the coming of the Reign of God that Jesus preached. Ministry is not the only way to facilitate the Reign of God however. It is one way among many. The enactment of just laws, medical breakthroughs, the revitalization of schools and neighborhoods, the creation of beautiful art and music, the rejuvenation of polluted waters are only a few ways that we may contribute to the reign of justice and peace. So too are visiting Grandma,

painting a friend's house and collecting money for a good cause.

Two cautions may be necessary here: First, the Reign of God is not the same as the establishment of an earthly state of justice and peace. The Reign of God will not be fully accomplished without that, but the good-life-for-all-here is not the whole story.

The second caution is that we do not alone bring about the Reign of God. That would be to fall into the fifth-century heresy of Pelagianism, which held that through their own efforts, human beings may gain salvation. In this, as in all things, we are dependent on the grace of God. God will effect the Reign. But even here we need to acknowledge that God alone will not do it. Mutual cooperation between God and creatures is necessary.

The vocation of the Christian is to be sent as the disciples of old to proclaim, celebrate, and serve the Reign of God. Ecclesiologist Richard McBrien sees this Reign of God "as broad and as overarching as the will of God is broad and overarching. In God, of course, everything is one. God is not separate from the will of God. If the [Reign of God] is the will of God in force, then [the Reign of God] is God."[1] When we minister for the coming of the Reign of God we are facilitating the communion of

Commisioning Laity
Catholic News Service

all of creation with our loving God. The traditional word vocation was thought to apply only to priests, sisters, and brothers. But every Christian is called to follow Christ. We might remember that when we pray for vocations.

Ecclesial or church ministry has long been the province of the ordained clergy. The laity were primarily responsible for ministering to the needs of the world. Those boundaries have begun to dissolve. Clergy are involved in political, economic, and social problems, and lay men and women perform a variety of professional church ministries.

Ministry to Institutions and Systems

The 1971 International Synod of Bishops proclaimed that "action on behalf of justice and participation in the transformation of the world fully appear to us as a constitutive dimension of the preaching of the Gospel, or in other words, of the church's mission for the redemption of the human race and its liberation from every oppressive situation." The demands of justice call us to minister to institutions, systems, and the culture as well as to individuals. The demands of justice are essential to the Gospel. We dare not ignore them.

The ministry of Jesus is a model for ministry to systems. While he healed and forgave, he also criticized and condemned injustice in the temple and in society. The passion and death of Jesus were the result of his challenge of evil. In our own century, Martin Luther King, Jr., Archbishop Romero, and the martyrs of El Salvador, Jean Donovan, Dorothy Kazel, Ita Ford, and Maura Clark, the six Jesuits and the two women killed with them are stark reminders of the consequences of taking the hard road.

The church has been criticized for a band-aid approach to ministry, bandaging wounds that should not have been inflicted in the first place. As a church, we have often been more responsive to individuals who suffer rather than to the cause of their suffering. It is as if attention paid to a person afflicted with a fatal disease were distracting us from searching for and eliminating the cause of the

disease. While we must continue to assist the immediate needs of poor and oppressed people, that cannot be the whole extent of our ministry. Even the most personal and individual ministry must be kept within the context of systemic oppression. We have to keep ministering to persons who are ill, but we also need to find out the cause of the illness.

In the following sections we will discuss ministry from the perspective of the laity and then the specialized ministries of ordained deacons, priests, and bishops. But before we speak of the ministry of the laity, it may be well to discuss what it means to be a lay woman or man in the church.

Who Are The Laity?

The Laity are the Church

When asked who the laity are, John Henry Newman replied, "The Church would look foolish without them." Indeed, we have to say that not only would the church look foolish but that there is no church without the laity. The hierarchy alone, important as they are, are not the church. The theologians at Vatican II understood this and incorporated the idea into several documents, especially *Gaudium et Spes* and *Apostolicam Actuositatem* (*Decree on the Apostolate of the Laity*). It is the first time in our history that any church council specifically addressed the topic of the laity. There were few precedents for the council fathers to draw from; they were, for the most part, breaking new ground.

That breaking of new ground included attempts at defining the laity positively. Common usage is reflected in the dictionary definition of the word *lay* as one who is not professional, not expert, not in orders, not clerical. It is one of the few words specified by what it is not. The theologians at the council provided another way of identifying lay persons in the church. Everything that is said of the People of God applies to the laity, including members of religious congregations and priests alike. Lay persons share in the priestly, prophetic, and kingly functions of Christ. We have moved somewhat from a negative understanding of the laity to a more positive one. Of course, the process is slow, but it has begun.

The universal call to holiness issued by the Council further breaks down the divisions between clergy and laity. Lay men and women are called to lives of holiness and sanctity just as clergy are. All Christians are called to the perfection of Christian life. This is not a call to be perfect in the sense of never making a mistake or an error; it is rather a call to be perfectly what we have been created to be — human and Christian.

This more positive conception of the laity is evident in the American bishops' pastoral letter on the laity, "Called and Gifted." They end their remarks with the words, "We have spoken in order to listen… We now await the next word." That next word is being spoken and lived out by the laity who are assuming responsibility for the transformation of the world and the church.

This American laity who speak the next word are different from the laity of other countries. According to a recent Gallup poll 43 percent of them attend church once a week or more, as compared with 21 percent of Germans, 12 percent of the French, and 3 percent of Danes.

There is another way that American lay people are different from those in other countries. Catholic lay folk, like other Americans (with the terrible exception of those persons who were forcibly brought here as slaves), come from people who sought liberation from poverty, hunger, religious and political oppression, and who hold "life, liberty and the pursuit of happiness" as among their rights given by God, not by the state or the church. They value democratic means of problem-solving and think they should have a voice in decisions that involve them. They are, of course, not alone in this, but it is one of their strong characteristics.

Our politicians know this. They call on God in political speeches, are photographed going to church or with prominent church leaders, thinking that the voters will be impressed. And often they are. For better and for worse, the connection between God and country is strong. This is not so much the case in European countries.

I am not trying to canonize the American laity; but simply attempting to bring some balance into the conversation. The charges of selfishness, greed, arrogance, and superiority that have been brought against Americans remind us that we still need conversion. But all is not negative. Sinners/saints that we are, occasionally we need to focus on the positive.

Toward an Understanding of the Laity

Therefore, the chosen People of God is one, "one Lord, one faith, one baptism" (Eph. 4:5). As members, they share the same dignity from their rebirth in Christ. They have the same filial grace and the same vocation to perfection. They possess in common one salvation, one hope, and one undivided charity. Hence, there is in Christ and in the church no inequality on the basis of race or nationality, social condition or sex, because "there is neither Jew nor Greek; there is neither slave nor free; there is neither male nor female. For you are all one in Christ Jesus" (Gal. 3:28).

Lumen Gentium, #32

Sisters and Brothers: Laity

It comes as a shock to some people that members of religious orders are lay persons unless they happen to be ordained to the priesthood. There is no intermediate step between laity and clergy in the church. All unordained persons are lay. That fact has not seeped into the Catholic consciousness. Even when it might be admitted that sisters are lay women, they are perceived as not quite like other lay women. A kind of pseudoclerical aura sometimes exists around persons in religious congregations.

Keeping the Original Vision

Although a founder might have been a woman of quite staggering courage and independence in her time, her modes of thought and behavior were bound to lose their pioneering flavor with the passing of centuries. But her community continued to cling to the old observances. So the original spirit of her order — the fearless innovation and the brave initiative — was lost, drowned in a welter of archaic absurdities: refectory regulations patterned on the eating habits of eighteenth-century French peasants, stilted recreational practices of a Victorian household, clothes of sixteenth-century Belgian widows.[2]

–Marcella Bernstein, *The Nuns*

The radical changes followed from Vatican II's invitation to religious congregations to become involved in two simultaneous processes. One was to return to Scripture, the source of all Christian life, and to the original inspiration of the founder. The other was to attend to the contemporary human condition and adjust to the changed conditions of the times. Repeating behaviors and practices of the past rather than keeping faithful to the vision of the founder left some religious congregations out of touch with the people they served.

Following the council's mandate to attend to the needs of the time, members of religious congregations took responsibility for new ministries both in the church and in society. Previously, the main ministry of sisters and brothers had been teaching children. Today, we are more likely to find them not only on parish or diocesan staffs and marriage tribunals, but also in prisons, homeless shelters, AIDS crisis centers, and even in political lobby organizations. Congregations

of women and of men are filled with sisters and brothers who wish to assume full adult responsibility in the church and the world.

The sweet little innocent girl-nun and the simpleton-brother (if they ever existed anywhere but in some people's imagination) are gone. The ogre sister or brother who used the paddle are also gone. Religious brothers had to contend with being almost invisible in the church, misunderstood because most people did not understand the distinction between brothers and priests. Brothers are men who have vowed poverty, celibacy, and obedience in a religious congregation but who have not presented themselves for ordination.

The Leadership Conference of Women Religious, the Conference of Major Superiors of Men, the National Black Sisters Conference, Las Her-manas, the National Assembly of Religious Women, and the National Coalition of American Nuns may differ in their goals, but they are fostering cooperation among congregations as well as focusing attention on the call to ministry.

The diminishing numbers of canonical religious has been a cause of concern to many Catholics. But one of the happy results of that decrease may be that lay women and men are assuming responsibility for what was once thought to be solely the province of members of religious congregations.

You may have noticed that I have tried to avoid using the noun "religious" when referring to brothers and sisters. If they own the word, then are other laity unreligious? Irreligious? A-religious? Discontinuing the use of the word is an attempt to place members of canonical congregations where they belong — as members of the laity.

Having specified what it means to belong to the laity, let us turn our attention to the call to minister as lay persons.

Laity As Ministers

Theology usually follows practice. The experience of the Christian community is what gives rise to theological reflection and development. Theology is reflection upon our experience of God; it is an effort to interpret, organize, and articulate that experience. Theology follows the events and circumstances of the Christian community in each age. Theologians investigate the issues that have arisen in the life of the church, put them in conversation with our tradition, and attempt to express them in a way that is faithful to the faith and responsive to current concerns.

Sisters Breaking Bread Together
Sisters of St. Joseph, Brentwood, NY

The *Decree on the Apostolate of the Laity* declares that each Christian is gifted by the Spirit and that those gifts are to be used in the church and in the world for the good of humanity and for the building up of the church (#3).

But Vatican II is ambivalent in its remarks about the laity. This is not unusual for documents written by different committees. On the one hand, it identified the laity as responsible for "christianizing the social order." On the other, the laity were called on to cooperate in "the apostolate of the hierarchy." The involvement of the laity in internal church affairs was perceived by the council to be an extension of the ministry of the hierarchy.

In both practice and theory, the church has moved

The Call of Lay Persons to Ministry

The laity derive the right and duty with respect to the apostolate from their union with Christ their head. Incorporated into Christ's Mystical Body through baptism and strengthened by the power of the Holy Spirit through confirmation, they are assigned to the apostolate by the Lord himself. They are consecrated into a royal priesthood and a holy people (cf. 1 Pet. 2:4–10) in order that they may offer spiritual sacrifices through everything they do, and may witness to Christ throughout the world. For their part, the sacraments, especially the most holy Eucharist, communicate and nourish that charity which is the soul of the entire apostolate...

From the reception of these charisms or gifts [of the Spirit], including those which are less dramatic, there arise for each believer the right and duty to use them in the Church and in the world for the good of humankind and for the upbuilding of the Church.

Decree on the Apostolate of the Laity, #3

radically from that position. At first, a very small number of lay persons assumed responsibility for professional church work. Some handled the finances or real estate; others oversaw public relations offices in dioceses. In a short time, however, lay persons had titles such as Director of Religious Education, Liturgy Coordinator, Music Minister, Hospital Chaplain, Campus Minister, and Spiritual Director. As the need for professional training became evident, universities and seminaries established programs for the education of these new ministers.

The primary locus of the laity's vocation and ministry is in the world. This is not to set up a false dichotomy between the church as sacred and the world as secular, but rather to describe the role of the vast majority of lay persons. The place where they find God and exercise their ministry is at the workplace, the market, the neighborhood. Some of the laity serve as volunteer ministers in the church and an even smaller number serve as professional ministers, but most Christians minister as secretaries, farmers, police officers, lawyers, doctors, ditch diggers, mothers, fathers, government officials, and teachers, to name but a few.

This recognition of the ministry of the laity as the transformation of the world is giving rise to a theology of work and a spirituality of the laity. Spirituality is not an imposition of prayer, meditation, and other so-called "religious acts." Spirituality has to do with the integration of one's faith and the daily circumstances of life; there is no extra added on. Indeed, *Gaudium et Spes* assures us that when we work we not only alter things and society, we develop ourselves as well. We learn much, we cultivate our resources, we go outside ourselves and beyond ourselves (GS, #35).

Many American Catholics have taken the challenge seriously and have become involved in ministry both in the church and to the rest of society. They have come to understand that "by its very nature the Christian vocation is also a vocation to the apostolate" (*Apostolate of the Laity*, #2). It is a startling thought: To be Christian is to be called to share in the mission of the church itself, to be responsible for the ministry of the church.

This is a far cry from an earlier understanding of the laity's involvement in Catholic action which was defined as "the collaboration of the laity in the apostolate of the hierarchy." The understanding of both the hierarchy and the laity was that when lay persons ministered, they were not responding to their own call to ministry but acting as aides in the ministry of the priests and bishops. The council has insisted that ministry is not the sole province of the hierarchy but the gift and responsibility of all.

Lay women and men minister in a variety of ways in parishes, hospitals, schools, and college campuses, not to mention such places as hospices, shelters for the homeless, and homes for battered women. They carry communion to the sick, are responsible for liturgy planning and preparation, proclaim the scriptures, and administer parishes. In some places where there are too few priests, lay persons conduct Sunday services, preach, baptize and preside at funeral services.

In Alaska, a bishop has given permission for a sister to witness marriages, because the weather often prevents priests from arriving on time. The extreme weather in that state has caused a joke to make the rounds that communal penance services are needed because for a sinner to fly to have venial sins forgiven is too expensive and for mortal sins, too dangerous.

In 1971, Pope Paul VI announced that the offices of lector and acolyte no longer were the province of seminarians but could be carried out by lay persons. In the same year, he reestablished the office of permanent deacon. Two years later, extraordinary ministers of the Eucharist were approved. As with most changes in the church, the pope was giving approval for practices that were already occurring in some places.

Canon 230 states that males may be commissioned to the ministries of lector and acolyte but that all lay persons may "fulfill the function of lector during liturgical actions by temporary deputation: likewise all lay persons can fulfill the functions of commentator or cantor or other functions, in accord with the norms of law."[3] Many dioceses and parishes have eliminated the commissioning ceremony because the ministry of women is not ritually recognized. In other places, both women and men are commissioned for their liturgical ministries.

Some parishes send ministers forth from the community each Sunday with a blessing. Religious educators are sent from the liturgy with a blessing as they go to teach the children; those who bring communion to the sick leave with the blessing of the community.

The practice of commissioning lay persons raises questions about the unintended effect of placing them in a clerical mode. Clericalizing a small number of the laity is not the model for lay ministry. Setting aside a few lay women and men from the rest of the community may introduce tensions unnecessarily. The question is not an easy one to settle.

Before we discuss the ministry of the ordained clergy, it may be well to remind ourselves once more that every baptized Christian is by virtue of that baptism called to ministry. The sacraments of Baptism and Confirmation are the sacraments of ministry. The sacrament of Orders is the sacrament that sets some Christians in a specialized ministry among the many ministries in the church. Another distinction to be remembered is that there is one sacrament of Orders that consists of three degrees: episcopate (bishops), presbyterate (priests) and diaconate (deacons).

Perhaps the most important thing to remember is that scholars generally agree that Jesus did not ordain anyone. Ordination is a development that occurred in the post-resurrection church.

Ministry Of The Ordained

Diaconate

Paul mentions deacons in some of his epistles, but they do not appear elsewhere in the New Testament. He uses the verb form of the word in describing himself as deacon; Stephanus and his co-workers, the first converts in Achaia, appear to be "bishops" because they are "deacons"; Timothy the deacon was a missionary; and Phoebe, patron and sister to Paul, is called deacon. The word *diakonos* may simply indicate those who had some positions of leadership in the early church. It is no wonder that Scripture scholars are not in agreement about the function of these deacons. However, there is great agreement that *diakonos* as used by Paul was not the precursor of today's deacons.[4]

By the fourth century, some deacons were powerful men, the right hand of the bishop making decisions about the daily running of the church. Other rural deacons worked in local congregations with priests, much as today's deacons do. Many factors contributed to the decline of the office of deacon by the year 1000. One factor may have been rivalry between priests and deacons over functions and leadership. Another was the rise of monasteries and

> ## Paul's Advice on Deacons
>
> Deacons likewise must be serious, not double-tongued, not indulging in much wine, not greedy for money; they must hold fast the mystery of faith with a clear conscience. And let them first be tested; then if they prove themselves blameless let them serve as deacons. Women [deacons] likewise must be serious, not slanderers, but temperate, faithful in all things. Let deacons be married only once, and let them manage their children and their households well; for those who serve well as deacons gain a good standing for themselves and great boldness in the faith that is in Christ Jesus.
>
> *1 Tim. 3:8–13*

Believe what you read; teach what you believe; practice what you teach.

Prayer said at the presentation of the Scriptures during the Ordination of Deacons

Diaconal Ordination
Holy Cross Mission Center

the establishment of orphanages and hospitals. Much of the pastoral ministry done by deacons was absorbed by monks and other lay folk and the deacon's role was limited to the liturgy.

The office of deacon was not totally abolished but by the time of the high Middle Ages, the diaconate was a temporary step along the road toward priesthood.

Women deacons appear to have been part of the clergy until around the sixth century. There are instructions for the laying on of hands for women deacons and indications that they were considered part of the clergy. Other documents that attest to their existence are those that tried to restrict their work. The First Council of Orange (441), for instance, provides this odd text: "Deaconesses are absolutely not to be ordained; and if there are still any of them, let them bow their heads under the benediction that is given to the congregation." A century later, the Second Council of Orleans (533) declared, "No longer shall the blessing of women deaconesses be given, because of the weakness of the sex."

Pope Paul VI restored the ancient order of diaconate in 1967. The promulgation of *Sacrum Diaconatus Quaedam* reestablished the permanent diaconate alongside the transitional diaconate to the priesthood.

While there are about 10,000 permanent deacons in the United States, it is disturbing to browse through books on the church and on ministry and to find that deacons are hardly mentioned at all. In some works on the church by major theologians they are not even listed in the index. Dismaying as that may be, it challenges the church to investigate some reasons for the slow acceptance of permanent deacons in some areas.

One explanation may be that in this country lay persons may carry out all of the roles that are assigned to deacons: they serve as Eucharistic ministers, conduct prayer services, and serve the pastoral needs of the community. They may, under special circumstances, preach, baptize, and witness marriages.

Other reasons may be the resistance of some of the clergy to accept clerics with wives and the resistance of the laity to accept a minister who is perceived to be "less than a priest."

Presbyters

In the Jewish community, priests were those who performed ritual sacrifices and who cared for the Temple. As Jews, Jesus and his disciples were familiar with the sacrificial nature of the priests' service. The early church would not have recognized their leaders as priests.

The word *priest* is used in the New Testament to refer only to Christ or to the whole body of Christians. The Epistle to the Hebrews presents Christ the "merciful and faithful high priest in the service of God" (2:17). The First Epistle of Peter encourages the community with the words, "But you are a chosen race, a royal priesthood, a holy nation, God's own people in order that you might proclaim the mighty acts of him who called you out of darkness into his marvelous light" (2:9).

Vatican II insists that ordained priesthood and the priesthood of all believers differs "in essence not only in degree" and that they are rooted in the one priesthood of Christ. The documents do not spell out the difference in essence and theologians have been researching that since the Council.

Priests are not or-

dained just to preside when the community is gathered to celebrate the Eucharist. They are responsible for the ministry of the Word and for the building up of the community. These three responsibilities are so mutually interdependent that they cannot be understood apart from one another. Sometimes the expectations we place on priests are overwhelming. But pastors and other clergy are not alone responsible for the mission of the church.

It may be too simplistic to say that priests are responsible for the formation of community, preaching the Word, and presiding at Eucharist. These roles get spelled out in myriad ways. Pastors are responsible for providing counselling for persons who are grieving, preparing couples for marriage, consoling the bereaved, healing fractures in the community, assuring the training of liturgical ministers, providing education for both children and adults in the parish, and encouraging and coordinating the ministries among church members.

Priests are also expected to prepare their homilies well so that the community may be nourished

The Ministerial Priesthood

Discipleship of Equals
Catholic News Service

And so, whether by honorable behavior among the nations they lead them to glorify God, whether by openly preaching they proclaim the mystery of Christ to unbelievers, whether they hand on the Christian faith or explain the church's teaching, or whether in the light of Christ they strive to deal with contemporary problems, the task of priests is not to teach their own wisdom but God's Word, and to summon all men [sic] urgently to conversion and to holiness (#4).

The office of pastor is not confined to the care of the faithful as individuals, but also as properly extended to the formation of a genuine Christian community (#6).

No Christian community, however, can be built up unless it has its basis and center in the celebration of the most Holy Eucharist. Here, therefore, all education in the spirit of community must originate. If this celebration is to be sincere and thorough, it must lead to various works of charity and mutual help, as well as to missionary activity and to different forms of Christian witness (#6).

Decree on the Ministry and Life of Priests

by the Word of God. But most importantly, priests are expected to preside at Eucharist and administer the other sacraments in such a manner that their dramatic and transforming power may be experienced by the community and that the whole community is enabled truly to participate in the celebration.

When American Catholics were asked what they wanted from their pastors, the number one response by a wide margin was "sensitivity to the needs of others."[5] Good preaching, learning, and organizational skills came in a far second, as did holiness. Perhaps sensitivity to the needs of others colors all the other characteristics of a good pastor.

Celibacy was not widely practiced in the early church. Presbyters, deacons, and bishops married and had children. The icon of Peter and his wife used by CORPUS, the organization of priests who are no longer in the active ministry, recalls that fact. By the fourth century there was a movement toward celibacy, in keeping with the then-current belief that all intercourse, even between married persons, was at least venially sinful and tolerated only for the procreation of children. Theology at that time held celibacy to be superior to marriage.

By the twelfth century, legislation required celibacy of the clergy; priests who were married had to leave their wives and children if they wanted to continue as ordained ministers. There was "relatively universal" observance in the following centuries.

Episcopate

Bishop is a modern term used to describe those ministers the early church called *episcopus*, a word that means "overseer." It was and is the function of the bishop to govern and administer the various local churches. But the local church is not the whole

What I am for you terrifies me; what I am with you consoles me. *For* you I am a bishop, but *with* you I am a Christian. The former is a title of duty; the latter one of grace. The former is a danger, the latter salvation. If, then, I am gladder by far to be redeemed *with you* than I am to be placed *over you*, I shall, as the Lord commanded, be more completely your servant.

–St. Augustine

story. The bishop as well as all Christians must be sensitive to the needs of the whole church. It is for this reason that we pray at Mass for the pope, the bishop, and "the entire people your Son has gained for you."

As the various heresies arose in the early church the bishops met together to defend the church. These meetings are the forerunners of today's synods where bishops of a region or country meet to confer on significant issues in the life of the church. Meetings of all the bishops of the world are a new phenomenon since Vatican II. Ecumenical councils are the most authoritative of bishops' meetings.

One of the greatest developments resulting from the council is the idea of collegiality. Collegiality is a mode of decision-making that is based on shared responsibility among a group. Because the church is a communion of local churches, authority is shared among the bishops. We speak now of the college of bishops, who in union with the pope exercises authority in national and regional conferences like the National Council of Catholic Bishops in the United States, in synods, and in ecumenical councils. Decision-making in a collegial mode has become more common in these later decades.

The American bishops meet twice yearly to address questions of concern for the church in the United States and for mutual support. It is as a result of these meetings that the bishops were able to address the issues of war and the economy already mentioned in the previous chapter.

While bishops are often referred to as the successors to the apostles, theologians and the hierarchy no longer unanimously defend the notion that there is a clear and direct line from Peter and the apostles to the pope and the bishops. Apostolic succession belongs not to individual bishops, nor even to the college of bishops but to the whole church.

Bishops are bishops because of ordination, not because of juridical mandate. While bishops are named by the pope, their office is "received through episcopal consecration." They are, at the same time, under the authority of the pope and "the proper, ordinary and immediate pastors" of their dioceses. They are not the pope's representatives or delegates but rather are "vicars and ambassadors of Christ."

Conclusion

Every Christian is called to ministry. In our day, lay men and women, priests, and deacons are learning to minister in the church in a collaborative way. In many places, the gifts of each are celebrated and used for the benefit of the community. The process is not an easy one, but for those who have committed themselves to it, nothing else is just or possible.

Notes

1. Richard McBrien, *Ministry: A Theological and Pastoral Handbook* (San Francisco: Harper & Row, 1986), 19.
2. Marcella Bernstein, *The Nuns* (Philadelphia: J.B. Lippencott, 1976), 235.
3. *Code of Canon Law: Latin-English Edition* (Washington, D.C.: Canon Law Society of America, 1983), 77.
4. See Lynn C. Sherman, *The Deacon in the Church* (New York: Alba House, 1983) for a more extensive discussion of the diaconate.
5. Notre Dame Study of Catholic Parish Life, 1984–1989.

6
Redefining the Community

When Jesuit Avery Dulles studied the documents of Vatican II, he discovered that the council used different models to describe the church. At times, they spoke of the institutional structure — the hierarchy, the rules and regulations that maintain the church. At other times, they referred to the church as community or as the herald of the Word of God. There was also a strong cry for the church to see itself as servant to individuals, to structures, and to the world. In addition, some documents pointed to the church as a sign or sacrament of God's presence in the world. Institution, community, herald, servant and sacrament — five ways we might think of church without any one of them taking precedence over or denying the validity of the others.

About twenty years after publishing those five models, Dulles suggested that there was one model that included all the others, and that was the model of discipleship. To be called to follow Jesus, to be his disciple, means to be called into the Christian community, to be responsible for the preaching of the gospel in both word and deed, and to minister to people in need. Moreover, it means living in such a way that God is made visible to others.

This discipleship requires some structure to maintain itself and to order the ministry of the community according to the gifts of the members. A collection of people, each doing his or her own thing, is not a community. Structure is a necessary part of any process, a lesson that some groups discovered when they rejected all structure because of their disillusionment with real or perceived abuses of authority.

Discipleship, then, is what we are about as church. Each individual Christian and the church at large is called to follow Jesus, to be disciple. Elisabeth Schüssler Fiorenza characterizes that discipleship as a discipleship of equals in which domination has no place.[1] Over and over, Jesus warned his followers against seeking the best seat at table, sitting at his right or left hand, and lording it over others. He insisted that they serve one another as he had served them; that they become even as the least in the community, a child. In his community, the first would be last and the last first.

When Peter asked Jesus what reward the disciples would receive for having left all things to follow him, Jesus assured them that "there is no one who has given up home, brothers, sisters,

Discipleship of Equals
Catholic News Service

mother or father, children or property, for me and for the gospel who will not receive in this present age a hundred times as many homes, brothers and sisters, mothers, children and property — and persecution besides — and in the age to come, everlasting life" (Mark 10:29–30). You will notice that fathers are not among the hundredfold promised. Fiorenza suggests that Jesus is renouncing patriarchal fatherhood in which one powerful man had the right to decide life-and-death issues for other men and for all women. The patriarch ruled over the extended family, the clan, and everyone in the family was subordinate to him. Not so among the disciples of Jesus.

"Call no one Father" is not a rejection of fatherhood as we know it today but may be understood as Jesus' renunciation of the patriarchal society prevalent in his day. The Fatherhood of God subverts the power of systems of domination and subordination. It condemns the exploitation of the poor, the powerless, and the outcasts.

Paul reinforces the idea of a discipleship of equals when he describes the post-resurrection community of Jesus in which "there does not exist among you Jew or Greek, slave or free, male or female. All are one in Christ Jesus" (Gal 3:28). The societal relationships of domination and subordination have no place among the disciples of Jesus. Jewish Christians are not to think themselves better than the converts from paganism; Christian masters are not to look down on slaves, and Christian men (even though they live in a patriarchal culture) are called on to accept women as their equals in Christ.

This call to a discipleship of equals is evident today in some developments among the laity. Adult Christian women and men are seeking to share their gifts, talents, ideas, and energy in the church. We can recognize a hunger for a discipleship of equals in the number of lay persons who are enrolled in seminaries and universities studying theology to prepare themselves better for ministry; in parish efforts to create ministerial teams that include lay women and lay men as well as clergy; in the expectation of the laity to be involved in decisions that affect their lives; and also in religious congregations that no longer use the language of "Mother or Father Superior" with its suggestion of a parent-child relationship.

Most of the developments in the past thirty or so years move toward a discipleship of equals, even if they are not described as such in so many words. The attraction of more egalitarian communities is a manifestation of our generation's longing for community. Complex as the reasons for that are, we might suggest that the mobility of our society with its fracturing of family and neighborhood relationships as well as the adult appropriation of the faith both contribute to the phenomenon.

As more lay men and women are involved in church affairs, they expect to be included in decision-making. Often where this is not possible in the traditional setting, they form alternative communities within the greater church. The groups that we will discuss are formed out of great love for the church, not in competition with it. They are witness to another face of the church.

Christian Communities Through the Ages

The phenomenon of small Christian communities that exploded on the scene in the past few decades has roots almost as old as Christianity itself. In each age, some people desired to live the Christian message in more radical ways than others. They searched for ways to live out the gospel message as they understood it.

The early hermits, for instance, who fled to the

The Fatherhood of God

The saying of Jesus uses the "father" name of God not as a legitimization for existing patriarchal power structures in society or church but as a critical subversion of all structures of domination. The "father" God of Jesus makes possible the "sisterhood of men" (in the phrase of Mary Daly) by denying any father, and all patriarchy, its right to existence. Neither the "brothers" nor the "sisters" in the Christian community can claim the "authority of the father" because that would involve claiming authority and power reserved for God alone.

–Elisabeth Schüssler Fiorenza
In Memory of Her

desert were, for the most part, lay women and men seeking a countercultural way of expressing their Christianity. There were historical events that led to the flight to the desert, not the least of which was the recognition of the church by Constantine and the eventual acceptance of Christianity as the official state religion.

As the church became respectable, some converts sought baptism as a means of social advancement; the hierarchy took on the trappings of royalty, Greek influences rather than Hebrew ones determined the theology that developed, and the institution became more involved with the very forces that had previously oppressed it. While it did affect those forces, it was itself affected by them. The institutional structure of the church began to resemble the structure of the state, and bishops began to be called "Princes of the Church." The government donated courts of justice, long buildings with a circular apse at one end to the church and that style of architecture determined the shape of church buildings for centuries.

Some Christians who were offended by this development believed that the best way to be Christian was to flee the world and live an ascetic life of penance. Many who went to the desert led heroic lives of prayer and penance but some, motivated by Gnostic tendencies that disdained the body, went to such extremes that their sanctity and even their sanity may be questioned.

The Flight to the Desert

At a later date, women and men who filled monasteries were also, for the most part, lay persons searching for a more radical approach to Christianity than most. This may be a good place to remind ourselves that there are only two categories in the church, laity and clergy; there is no half step in between for members of religious congregations.

A particularly interesting group developed in the twelfth century that in some ways resembles the contemporary Charismatic movement. The *Humilitati* or "Humble Ones," discouraged by the lack of relevance of some preaching, encouraged their members to preach. Since preaching was declared to be the province of the clergy, they were forbidden to continue by Pope Alexander III in 1179. Five years later, they were condemned by Lucius III. But in 1201, Innocent III found a compromise that permitted them to continue their ministry of the Word. Innocent made a distinction between preaching in the area of doctrine (*articuli fidei*) which was the province of the clergy and exhorting others to lead a life of piety (*verbum exhortationis*), which could be the work of the laity.

Early Lay Preaching

In the Low Countries, the twelfth century also saw the establishment of a community of lay women called Beguines. Beguines were women who wanted to live a more integrated Christian life and who did not wish to join a convent or monastery. They took no public vows, were not enclosed in a cloister, worked among the people of the town or city, and lived simply, sometimes at home with their families and sometimes in a small group. The radical nature of their life can be understood when we remember that at that time all nuns were cloistered. The first of the so-called "active orders" had not yet been established. While some clergy supported their endeavors, some were suspicious of women who were not protected by cloister and vows. Beguines were often accused of heresy by their adversaries but, more recently, they have been called the first Christian women's movement.

It appears that there have always been Christian women and men who rejected some of their society's values and sought ways to live a more radical Christianity. In all cases, that meant searching for a community that would support and encourage that radical living. Ancient documents give evidence that even the desert mothers and fathers, solitary as their lives were, had the support of others who fled to the desert. It should also be remarked that the numbers of these Christians were always small. Most Christians did not go to the desert; most did not enter monasteries or convents; most did not join the *Humilitati* or the Beguines. But some did, and they had a profound effect on the rest of the church.

Radical Twentieth-Century Communities

In this century, the search for a more intense way to follow gospel values has given rise to a wide variety of communities. As in the past, the focus has been on prayer and service to a broken society. The pattern is not to flee the world, however, but to live out gospel values in the everyday circumstances of life.

In the 1930s, a socialist and former communist sympathizer chose to be baptized Catholic. It was not an easy move; it would mean that she could no longer live with her lover, would lose many of her friends, and be part of a church that she recognized as not living up to the radical demands of the gospel. Yet, finding herself at home in such a church, she searched for some way to live out her commitment to the poor as Catholic. Her meeting with a wise but eccentric Peter Maurin provided her with the outlet she needed. Her first project was a newspaper sold for a penny on May Day in 1933 at a socialist and communist rally in New York's Union Square. So began Dorothy Day's odyssey.

This was the beginning of what became known as the Catholic Worker Movement — houses of hospitality where hungry people have both body and soul nourished and healed. Catholic Worker communities nourished not only the poor guests but generations of intellectuals and young activists. A simple lifestyle, prayer, liturgy, stimulating discussions on a wide range of topics, as well as food for the body are the hallmarks of Catholic Worker houses.

Around the same time, Catherine de Hueck opened Friendship House in Harlem, New York, modeled on one she had established in Toronto. Her work for social justice especially in the area of race relations attracted many young people who lived and worked in the interracial houses and farms that spread throughout the country. Their mode of radical gospel living included providing food and clothing for poor people.

But, like Catholic Workers, they went beyond that. They understood that in order to eliminate discrimination and injustice, society must change. To this end, they lectured, wrote, and conducted workshops on justice issues. They realized that the problem must be addressed on another level and attempted to change government structures by lobbying and nonviolent demonstrations.

Women's Groups

Some small Christian communities are composed of women who are struggling to maintain their relationship with the institutional church but who find that they must seek spiritual nourishment outside the traditional settings. They meet to discuss

Dorothy Day
Archives of the Congregation of the Holy Cross

Dorothy Day, Social Justice Prophet

We must minister to people's bodies in order to reach their souls. We hear of the faith through our ears, we speak of it through our mouths. The Catholic Worker Movement, working for a new social order, has come to be known as a community which breaks bread with brothers of whatever race, color or creed. "This is my body," Christ said at the Last Supper, as He held out bread to His apostles. When we receive the Bread of life each day, the grace we receive remains a dead weight in the soul unless we cooperate with that grace. When we cooperate with Christ, we work with Christ, in ministering to our brothers.

Dorothy Day, October 1940

and pray about the role of women in society and the church and to support one another in their spiritual journey.

Sadly, some groups of women have become separatists, finding the institutional structure too sexist to merit their loyalty. Lost to the church is their critical analysis and their creative imagination. Others maintain their ties to both the small group and to the parish, building bridges from one to the other.

One of the earliest and noncanonical women's groups is a movement that began in Europe. The Grail came to America in 1944. As a group of women without a clear relationship or responsibility to the hierarchy, they were viewed with some suspicion. One archbishop found their program sound but declared, "We cannot forget that they are a group of women being led by a woman, with a great deal of female emotions and instincts guiding them."[2]

They were at first influenced by their Jesuit founder who defined all the evils in society as "ultra masculine" as they sought to Christianize society with "a feminine character." One of the early conferences in 1954 was designed as an antidote to Simone de Beauvoir's feminism. At that time, they described Eve as naturally receptive and dependent and suited only for work in the home. In less than ten years, Grail members were in the forefront of Christian feminism.

Their commitment to the transformation of the world is evident in the retreats, workshops, conferences, and seminars that are conducted for women. Their members are single, married, and members of religious congregations; some are fully committed, others are described as still searching. Since 1962, Grail has accepted both Catholic and Protestant women.

Grail women were pioneers in the liturgical movement. Liturgy was the heart of their life and work and their celebrations involved both creativity and respect for the tradition. Like other liturgical pioneers, they made strong connections between liturgy and justice in the world.

Catholic Action

Not all movements were lay inspired. The hierarchy gave strong support to "Catholic Action." Catholic action was an effort on the part of bishops and priests to train the small groups of laity to assume responsibility for transforming the face of the earth. Catholic Action was defined as "the participation of the laity in the apostolate of the hierarchy." While it began as a clergy-sponsored program, it soon took on the character of an independent lay movement, understanding its ministry not as an extension of the hierarchy's but as its own Christian responsibility.

One of the differences between this movement and the others discussed above was that members were not required to leave their homes, families, and workplace. They met weekly to "observe, judge and act." Observing a particular situation and judging it in the light of the gospel required action on their part. "Action" was part of their name, and they were committed to renewing the face of the earth. Young Christian Students, Young Christian Workers, and the Christian Family Movement grew out of Catholic Action groups.

Not all groups that affected the lives of American women and men developed on this continent. During World War II, a small group of men, disturbed by the factions and divisions that tore the Body of Christ apart, dedicated themselves to living in a community that would be open to all. They wanted to provide a place of prayer for themselves and for others that would also serve as a house of hospitality for anyone who came to their door. They found that place in a house owned by one of their number, Roger Schutz, in Taizé, France. Over the years, Jews fleeing Nazis, refugees, and more recently, students have turned Taizé into a synonym for Christian unity. Men from different denominations call each other Brother and live as if there were no division in the church. Their lives attract thousands of young people, including many Americans, every year to a week of prayer, meditation, and liturgy that focuses on unity and peace.

While the lay movements discussed here are

often presented in the context of social justice, they also are the forerunners of the small Christian communities that exist today. Their concerns for prayer, community and Christian ministry and their ancient and new way of being church are mirrored in what has come to be known as the phenomenon of small Christian communities.

Small Christian Communities

These small Christian communities are known by a variety of names: basic Christian communities (BCCs), basic ecclesial communities (CEBs), communidades de base. Indeed, hundreds of labels are attached to them, but the predominant one is basic Christian communities.

The mushrooming of small Christian communities especially in Latin America and Africa has occurred in tandem with the development of liberation theologies. It is difficult, if not impossible, to determine which came first. Liberation theology grew out of the reflected-upon experiences of small communities, but small communities formed as theology developed that helped them to understand themselves. Groups of Christians who gathered to read Scripture and to put it in conversation with the events of their lives have assumed responsibility for being church and for working toward transforming society in accord with the good news of the Gospels.

While the focus of the small Christian communities that proliferate in the United States differs from the ones just mentioned, they share with them the deep concern to live the message of the gospel in a more profound way. They are more often composed of middle-class people rather than the very poor as in the so-called third-world countries. Although a keen sense of social justice is often the burning issue that brings them together, more emphasis is focused on the life of the community itself. In either case, these intentional communities are groups of persons who seek both support and challenge from other Christians. They seek to incarnate what it means to be church in a way other than the traditional parish.

Not all coming together of Christians are BCCs. Those groups that do not aspire to become, in themselves, a manifestation of church belong to more traditional forms of church. Parish staffs, sodalities, church societies, and clubs are constituted in such a way as to carry out a part of the mission of the larger church. They may come together to pray and to minister but they do not, in themselves, propose to become truly church.

Basic Christian communities attempt to incarnate some of what we know about the early Christian communities. The Jerusalem church called itself the *ekklēsia* of God (1 Cor. 15:9; Gal. 1:13). *Ekklēsia* meant the assembly of a political community. It also came to mean the chosen People of God. The early Christians also referred to themselves as "the saints" (Acts 9:13; Rom. 15:25). Both the largely Jewish Christian community in Palestine and the largely Gentile Christian communities started by the missionaries saw themselves and each other as the People of God.

The concept of "People of God" serves to eliminate an individualistic notion of sanctity and righteousness. Paul's letters are meant for the community; his words speak to the community. Individual salvation is not what Christianity is about.

We read that the early Christians "devoted themselves to the apostles' instruction and the common life, to the breaking of bread and prayers" (Acts, 2:42). Moreover, they sold what they had and shared according to each one's need (Acts, 2.46). Common life, hearing the Word, liturgy and service define the early church and so the church today. These four characteristics have traditionally been spoken of in their Greek forms: *koinonia, kerygma, leitourgia, and diakonia.*

Koinonia or community presumes mutuality, concern for the lives of members. It requires honest interaction — sometimes consoling and sometimes challenging. While friendship and fellowship make community delightful, koinonia is not friendship; it includes friendship but it is more. It is based on relationship in Christ, a shared discipleship, a gift of the Spirit. As such, it is neither simple nor easy.

Koinonia also demands relationships among small communities and with the greater church. Free-floating groups unattached in any way to the church tend to become sects, self-absorbed and self-destructive.

Koinonia or community as understood here does not fit neatly into categories devised by sociologists when they speak of primary groups and secondary groups. Primary groups include family and friends and are based on strong affective and emotional ties. That presumes a small enough number that face-to-face relationships are possible. Secondary groups are those in which the primary concern is not some purpose other than their interpersonal relationships.

The communities we are discussing here lie somewhere in between these two, sharing in the concerns of both. They are small enough for personal relationships to flourish, but if that were the main focus of attention, we would hardly call them basic Christian communities. They must also reach out to others to be truly Christian.

Community is not about navel-gazing; the main focus is not the good of the members or the creation of warm feelings among the group. Indeed, community is often a by-product of praying together, sharing one another's burdens, and reaching out corporately to others. It is what may happen when people stop thinking of themselves and their own needs. Groups that come together for the sole purpose of "making community" are often disillusioned.

Kerygma or the proclamation of the gospel provides the foundation of small Christian communities. The search for community, the service performed, and even the liturgy celebrated are firmly rooted in the gospel. Scripture reading and reflection connects personal and communal conversion as well as ecclesial renewal to biblical sources.

Leitourgia or the public celebration of liturgy involves both the liturgy of the Word and the liturgy of the Eucharist. Individual members may pray often and well, but it is the communal prayer that sustains the members.

Diakonia is the fourth mark of church. To be church, a group must not only form care for the members, root itself in the good news and celebrate liturgy together. They must live out the gospel of Jesus as they understand it and that involves balancing care for members by service to those outside the community. This includes ministry to individuals in need and service to the structures and institutions that may need transformation. Giving a glass of water in Jesus' name is good, but we may have to ask why people are thirsty. Diakonia includes both personal and societal ministry, giving the water and digging wells or installing water mains.

Another way of thinking of koinonia, kerygma, leitourgia, and diakonia is given by the formula 3W plus S equals C. Word, worship, witness of life, and service — all are involved in the everyday life of the church. Without God's Word, without liturgy and prayer, without the daily living of the gospel and without ministry to the poor and needy, there is no church.

From Catholic Action to Call to Action

In October 1976, the year of the American bicentennial celebration, more than 1,300 delegates met in Detroit for the "Call to Action" conference. The conference was conducted under the auspices of the National Conference of Catholic Bishops, and one-third of the members were named by the bishops. In preparation for the conference, regional meetings allowed interested Catholics to raise issues they thought ought to be addressed. They generated more than 800,000 suggestions.

The conference participants sent 182 of these recommendations to the bishops. Some of the resolutions concerned optional celibacy for priests, acceptance of artificial contraception, diocesan financial accountability, racism in the church, lay participation in decision-making, and the right of divorced Catholics to remarry. The delegates also called for more attention to the needs of families and for the renewal of parish life.

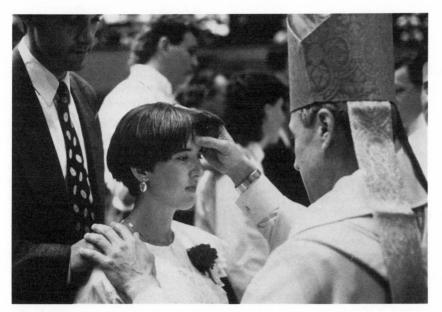

Gift of the Spirit
Catholic News Service

In 1966, a group of professors and students at Duquesne University in Pittsburgh began to meet for prayer and Scripture study. They were attracted by the power of the Pentecostal movement after reading David Wilkerson's *The Cross and the Switchblade*. In early 1967, some members asked the group to pray that they might be baptized in the Holy Spirit. One of them immediately began to pray in tongues. This baptism in the Spirit is the way the profound personal experience of the Spirit's presence in a person's life is sometimes described.

While Call to Action began as a program conducted by the bishops, after rejecting many of the resolutions, they voted to disband the group. But a group of Chicago Catholic women and men restructured the organization and have been working since for church reform and social justice. They publish a newsletter, network with other peace and justice groups, and have a theater group that travels around the country. The Call to Action Performing Arts Ministry brings the social justice agenda to the attention of audiences. The membership of Call to Action now spans the country.

The Charismatic Renewal

Since the late nineteenth century, Protestant Pentecostal churches took as their model the experience of the early community in the Acts of the Apostles after Pentecost. Literally following those early disciples, they prayed in tongues and developed an emotional style of worship focused on the presence of the Holy Spirit among them. Pentecostals were not part of mainline Protestant churches nor were there any Catholic Pentecostals.

Wanting to share their experience with other faculty and students, the group planned a weekend retreat. The now famous "Duquesne Weekend" saw about thirty students and faculty become more demonstrative and effusive in their prayer. Their unrestrained responses were out of character for academic types, but they were the beginnings of what has become the Catholic Charismatic Movement.

At first, not surprisingly considering the academic network, the movement spread among campuses in the midwest, including Notre Dame and Michigan State University. The number of Charismatic groups grew and soon thousands began to come together each year at the University of Notre Dame for their annual convention.

Charismatic groups usually meet for weekly prayer sessions that may last a few hours. Prayer and Scripture are the backbone of the meetings, accompanied by personal testimonies concerning the work of the Spirit in an individual's life. These meetings might include speaking and singing in tongues, laying hands upon the sick for healing, and baptism in the Spirit. Older devotions such as novenas often focus on sin and the sufferings and death of Jesus. The focus here is on the gifts of the Spirit, Christ, and on the possibility of sanctity for women and men.

The gifts of the Spirit or charisms that are celebrated in these communities are often accompanied by strong emotions. As with any movement that appeals strongly to the emotions, charges of anti-intellectualism and elitism are often raised. Some Charismatic groups are also criticized for an authoritarian style of leadership and their conservative views concerning the role of women in society and in the church.

Parish Life

It would be a mistake to think that all of the vibrant movement in the church is happening outside the traditional structures. More Catholics belong to parishes rather than to any of the groups we have just discussed. The revitalization of the church is occurring in and through dioceses and parishes in programs like RENEW, Genesis 2, and Christ Renews His Parish. RENEW has been part of the revitalization of more than a third of Catholic parishes. Groups in many parishes continue to meet for prayer and discussion even after the program has ended. But perhaps the most significant

---

The Catechumenate

The initiation of catechumens takes place step by step in the midst of the community of the faithful. Together with the catechumens, the faithful reflect upon the value of the paschal mystery, renew their own conversion and by their example lead the catechumens to obey the Spirit more generously.

Introduction to the revised Roman Ritual, #4

---

renewal of parishes has occurred through the Rite of Christian Initiation of Adults (RCIA).

Rite of Christian Initiation of Adults

The Rite of Christian Initiation of Adults is not technically a program; it is the way new members are welcomed into the Catholic communion. The process, from beginning to end, is a rite of the church. Although the bishops at Vatican II called for the restoration of the catechumenate, the period of formal preparation for entrance into the church, they were only responding to what some local churches had already been doing.

In some areas, a process of preparation for baptism that was based on the early practice of the church had already been inaugurated. No longer did a potential convert meet with a priest and study the doctrines and beliefs of the Catholic Church (perhaps in catechism form). They were, instead, initiated into the life of the community and learned from the community what it meant to be a Catholic Christian. It was this ancient and more recent form of initiation that finally became the present Rite of Christian Initiation of Adults.

In the early church, persons interested in becoming Christian went through a period called the catechumenate, which involved information, formation, and transformation. Instruction in Christian beliefs — doctrines, traditions, and rituals — aided Christian formation. The community was involved and responsible for the expected transformation into life in Christ. The catechumenate lasted sometimes three or more years. Slowly, the catechumen was incorporated into the life of the community and learned what it means to be Christian from that community. The process was geared to enliven the faith of the community even as it prepared the catechumen.

When the church became the official religion of the realm and mass conversions were the norm, the process of the catechumenate fell into disuse. The sacraments of initiation (Baptism, Confirmation, and Eucharist), originally bestowed together, were celebrated at different times in a person's life.

Infant baptism became the usual entry into the Christian community.

The RCIA is a return to the more ancient practice. As it has been structured, the RCIA begins with a period of inquiry during which interested persons meet one another, share their faith journey, and ask questions about the church. At this point, participants are called inquirers. They are accompanied on their journey by sponsors.

Those who decide to continue their journey toward baptism are welcomed by the community at the Rite of Entrance (also called the Rite of Welcome) into the Catechumenate. While local circumstance may require other timelines, this ritual blessing and invitation ordinarily occurs at the beginning of the church year on the first Sunday of Advent. From this Sunday until their baptism, the catechumens are dismissed from Mass after the liturgy of the Word. They meet together with their sponsors to reflect on the day's Scripture readings and other facets of Catholic belief.

There is no fixed period of catehumenate at this time, although most catechumens begin the final period of preparation during the Rite of Election on the first Sunday of Lent. The church officially welcomes those who will be baptized at Easter. The forty days of Lent is the period of final preparation. Now called "the elect" since they have been chosen or elected to receive the sacraments, the catechumens pass through the Period of Purification and Enlightenment. During these six weeks, catechumens are encouraged to pray, reflect on their lives and try to discover how they might develop a more loving relationship with God. The community joins the elect in those prayers and in reflection on its own life.

Finally, at the Easter Vigil, in the midst of sacramental fire, incense, oil, water, light, dark, music, processions, bread and wine, the candidates are initiated into the sacramental community and receive Baptism, Confirmation and Eucharist. On this holiest of nights new life in Christ is celebrated as the community witnesses the Baptism and renews its own baptismal promises.

Communities that have the RCIA have experienced a revitalization of faith far beyond that of the newly baptized and their sponsors. This is, in part, because the RCIA does not technically end at Easter. The period of fifty days until Pentecost are a model of how the community is meant to live always. This period of *Mystagogia* or mystery calls for a deepening of faith as the community together listens to the Word of God and celebrates the Eucharist.

The Universal Call to Holiness

Thus it is evident to everyone that all the faithful of Christ of whatever rank or status are called to the fullness of the Christian life and to the perfection of charity...

All of Christ's faithful, therefore, whatever be the conditions, duties and circumstances of their lives, will grow in holiness day by day through these very situations, if they accept all of them with faith and from the hand of their heavenly Father, and if they cooperate with the divine will by showing everyone through their earthly activities the love with which God has loved the world.

Lumen Gentium, (#40, 41)

The Call of the Whole Church to Holiness

When I was a child, my mother would often send a small donation to the Carmelite sisters to pray for her intentions. She was convinced that they were holier than she and that God would hear their prayers more readily. Sanctity, in popular opinion, was the province of the clergy, monks, religious sisters, and brothers. Ordinary Catholics hoped for salvation; very few thought that they were called to sainthood.

The universal call to holiness issued in *Lumen*

Holiness in the World

In nothing has the Church so lost her hold on the laity as in her failure to understand and respect the secular vocation. She has allowed work and religion to become separate departments, and is astonished to find that, as a result, the secular work of the world is turned to purely selfish and destructive ends, and that the greater part of the world's intelligent workers have become uninterested in religion. But is it astonishing? How can anyone remain interested in a religion which seems to have no concern with nine-tenths of life?

The Church's approach to a carpenter is usually confined to exhorting him not to be drunk and disorderly in his leisure hours, to come to Church on Sundays. What the Church should be telling him is this: that the very first demand that his religion makes upon him is that he should make good tables. Church, by all means; and decent forms of amusement, certainly. But what use is all of that if in the very center of his life and occupation he is insulting God with bad carpentry? No piety in the worker will compensate for work that is not true to itself; for any work that is untrue to its own technique is a living lie.[3]

–Dorothy Sayers, "Creed or Chaos"

Gentium began to change all that. It proclaims that holiness is not for the few but is the ordinary way for all Christians. Every Christian is called to a life of holiness and sanctity. Moreover, this holiness will promote a more human way of life (LG, #40). This connection between holiness and a more human way of living signals a radical shift in the church's attitude toward the world. Sanctity is not to be found in fleeing and rejecting the world but in making it more human, more holy.

The recent surge of interest in spiritual direction and in retreats is a clear sign of how seriously women and men have taken this call to holiness. It is also a sign that they realize that holiness is not an individualistic process but a communal one. We should also note the number of lay spiritual directors or spiritual companions who walk with both the laity and clergy, and conduct retreats and prayer days.

This is not to say that prayer and spiritual direction are the only way, or even the primary way to holiness. In fact, if prayer and spiritual direction get in the way of a person's life responsibilities, then we must wonder about their efficacy. Christian spirituality is about the integration of life; we become saints by relating all facets of life to God. Family, neighborhood, work, church, politics, economics, leisure — all contribute to the holiness of life. All are related; all are sacraments of God's presence.

The universal call to holiness does not only mean that every Christian is called to saintliness. It also means that every aspect of every life is able to contribute to bringing about the Reign of God in our world. This universal aspect of holiness is another example of what it means to be Catholic. Nothing is outside the purview of God's graceful presence among us.

Notes

1. Elizabeth Schüssler Fiorenza, *In Memory of Her: A Feminist Theological Reconstruction of Christian Origins* (New York: Crossroad, 1988), 151.
2. Quoted in Mary Jo Weaver, *New Catholic Women* (San Francisco: Harper & Row, 1985), 125.
3. Quoted by Joseph Cardinal Bernardin, in "Executives Must Practice Religious Beliefs at Work," in *One Body: Different Gifts, Many Roles* (Washington, D.C.: NCCB, 1987), 21.

7

The Church in America and the Universal Church

Conversations about church usually wind up focusing on the local parish or the Vatican. They might be about innovative programs that the parish council is encouraging, the renovation of the church building, the pastor's sermon, even fund-raising and Bingo games. Or the conversation may turn on some recent announcement from Rome (usually reported in the daily paper), papal visits, or the pageantry of the televised Christmas Mass and papal blessing.

Two faces of the same church, so distinct yet intimately united. For Catholics, the one does not make sense without the other. The local church and the universal church give meaning to each other, thereby helping us to understand what church truly is.

The church is one. The church is local. The church is universal. The church is the Body of Christ, the temple of the Holy Spirit, a mystery or sacrament "imbued with the hidden presence of God." At the same time, the church is many, including all who profess faith in Jesus Christ. The communion of local congregations constitutes the universal church.

Pre–Vatican II images of church were often described in terms of a pyramid. The pope, of course, was at the top with the cardinals just below, then the bishops, followed by the clergy on a lower level. The "faithful" were at the bottom. The pyramid was described from the top down. We rarely heard anyone say that the laity were the base, the firm foundation, the necessary underpinning of the whole. Action and communication flowed from the top down, not from the bottom up. It was an image that in another era seemed to serve the church well enough.

But as democratic principles filtered through society, including the church, and since Vatican II defined the church as the People of God, the pyramid alone was not sufficient to describe the church. More circular images were used. One image had the pope in the middle and the cardinals, bishops, priests, and laity in concentric circles, somehow suggesting that action flowed toward the center and from the center. Another had a circle cut up rather like a pizza representing one church divided into dioceses. But neither quite captured the meaning of the church as described by the council. The church is not centered on the pope, important as his role is, nor is it one great entity cut up into geographic units called dioceses.

Perhaps the one diagram that comes closest to describing the relationship between the local and the universal church is a circle with many smaller circles within. The great circle is church because it is composed of the many local churches. The distinction is important. The universal church is constituted by the communion of all the local churches, not the other way around. It is not that the local church absorbs its meaning from the universal church.

The model of the early churches, many and distinct from one another as they were, suggests that as the churches became more numerous it was necessary for some structure to hold them together and to insure fidelity to the apostolic teachings. The churches in Jerusalem, Antioch, Ephesus, Colossae, Galatia, Rome, and elsewhere established a network that eventually developed into a more solid and centralized organization. The communion of local churches became the universal church.

"The church" does not mean only the Roman Catholic Church. The phrase is also used to refer to the Eastern churches in union with Rome. They are called churches and not only Rites as they had previously been known. This change of language acknowledges that they have an integrity of their own. Calling them "Rites" seemed to indicate that the only difference between them and Catholics called Roman was the use of a different language in their liturgies. Liturgical language, however, is not the only difference. Eastern churches enjoy their own traditions, spirituality, history, and way of life, even as Roman Catholics do. No church is superior to the other by reason of rite; the Roman rite does not enjoy any kind of precedence over the other Catholic rites.

The council not only recognized other Catholic rites as "church," it also used the word to refer to other denominations. The communion of churches does not refer only to the communion of local congregations of the Roman Catholic Church and the Eastern churches in union with Rome, but also to churches of other Christian denominations. The church is the Body of Christ embracing all baptized Christians. The church is Orthodox, Oriental, Anglican, Protestant, and Catholic. For the first time, the Second Vatican Council referred to Anglican and Protestant denominations as "church."

Talk of local churches, the universal church, the various denominations as church may appear to be in conflict with one another, but they are all true according to the documents of the Second Vatican Council. Stretching the notion of church to include all branches of Christianity may be difficult for some to accept because we have often reserved the word to mean either the church of Rome or the local parish. But the church includes all those who profess faith in Jesus Christ.

We can say, then, that your local parish is church. Your diocese is church. The Lutheran church down the block is church. The Episcopal Church is church. The Greek Catholic Church is church. The Vatican is church.

Even though we say the church is one, we have to admit the scandalous divisions that exist among the various manifestations of church. In the next chapter we will discuss the efforts being made in the area of ecumensim.

Of course, not everyone who says, "Lord, Lord" enters the kingdom of heaven. So, too, not every group that professes belief in Jesus constitutes a church. Ecclesiologist Richard McBrien in his classic work, *Catholicism*[1], provides six criteria by which we might recognize these local manifestations of church. They are confession in the Lordship of Jesus, ratification of that confession sacramentally in Baptism, Eucharist (and other sacraments), openness to the Word of God as found in Scripture, a

"One Church, Many Models"

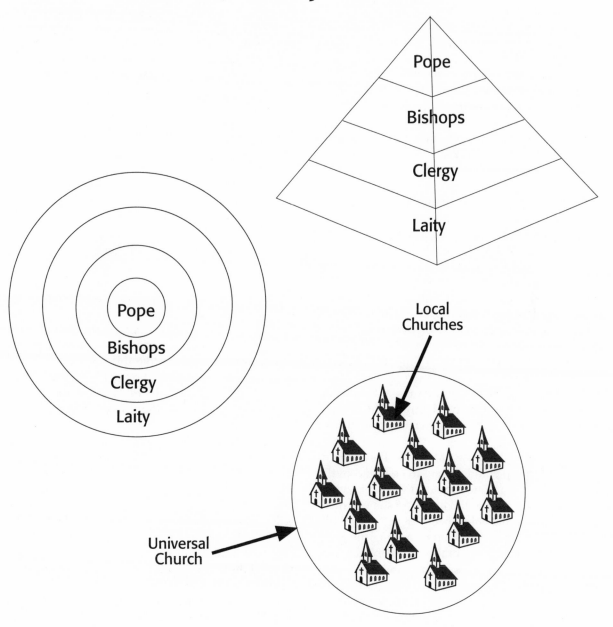

Pope

Bishops

Clergy

Laity

Pope
Bishops
Clergy
Laity

Local
Churches

Universal
Church

sense of community, willingness to live by gospel values and some form of ministry to insure stability and structure.

These criteria are not meant to impose some kind of uniformity on members of the various churches, nor are they an attempt to identify specific customs and behaviors by which church is to be recognized. Indeed, they allow for magnificent variety as Christians of the diverse cultures of the world express their faith in Jesus Christ in sacrament, community, Scripture, and ministry. This diversity does not manifest itself only in the different Christian denominations but also within the Roman Catholic Church itself.

We have discussed how the experience of living in the United States of America has shaped and colored our practice of Catholicism. Even within our borders, we notice great differences among Catholics — not only so-called conservative and liberal Catholics but even East coast, West coast, and middle American Catholics; Catholics of Italian or Irish descent, black Catholics, Hispanic Catholics. Our discussion in chapter two gave some appreciation of how the culture of a people affects their expressions of faith. That is an import-ant point: We share one faith that is affected by the culture and that is expressed in myriad ways. Catholicism is not monochromatic, producing light of only one wavelength, but a wonderful spectrum of many hues.

However great those variations, they pale in the face of the splendid variety to be found in the Catholic Church around the world. We will review, briefly, how the culture and history of some of these Catholics form and color their practice of Catholicism in other countries. Understanding the great diversity in customs, celebrations, and expressions of faith may lead to a more profound concept of what it means to be Catholic. We might even be able to echo the words of Irish novelist James Joyce, who in his own unique style said that Catholic means "Here comes everybody."

The Churches Around the World

It used to be said that wherever Catholics travelled they would be at home in any Catholic church. The language of the Mass was the same everywhere; the gestures and vestments of the priests were the same; the response of the congregation the same. That is not the case today. Although Catholics around the world treasure their common faith, stark differences in history and culture, and thus in rituals and celebrations, set them apart from one another.

In spite of our shared history, various developments in the United States have resulted in a broad spectrum of views on the church. What, then, can be said of the rest of the world? The church is affected in each locale by the art, music, politics, economy, geography, and history of the people. Each culture leaves its imprint on the church; each culture enriches it even as it is enriched; each culture challenges it even as it is challenged. The conversation goes in both directions, and both the culture and the church are affected by it.

While the church universal is the communion of local churches, that communion does not imply uniformity. In a study like this one, we are only able to make passing mention of the profound differences that make up the Body of Christ. Learning about churches in other places may help us to understand better what it means to belong to the universal church. Karl Rahner, preeminent among theologians, predicted that the church of the future will be "a world church, in which the Churches of Africa, South America and even Asia, will really be autonomous elements in the whole Church."[2] They will not look like Roman churches transplanted into other continents.

We might recall Gustavo Gutiérrez's assessment of the Second Vatican Council as a council of "the church in the modern world." It was not a council that enjoyed significant input from the Third World or even addressed the issues and problems of the Third World or the communist Second World as seriously as it did the concerns of the developed First World. Given the times and the purpose of the council, this is not surprising. The fact is, however, that the so-called second- and third-world churches are struggling to define themselves in the post–Vatican II church, each from the perspective of its own history and culture.

In 1960, more than half the world's Catholics lived in Europe or North America. Futurists predict that by the year 2000, only about 30 percent will be found there. The church appears to be migrating to the south and gaining strength among poorer and younger peoples and among peoples who are in the first stages of moving from colonialism to more democratic forms of government. Radical and dramatic changes in societies and therefore in the church accompany this development. It is a time when the call to be Catholic opens the church to exciting and challenging new developments.

"Catholic" means comprehensive, universal, all-inclusive. This inclusivity led Karl Barth, the great twentieth-century Protestant theologian, to say that his problem with Roman Catholicism is "and." His difficulty arises from the Protestant claim of "sola fides, sola scriptura, sola gratia" (faith alone, Scripture alone, grace alone). For Catholics it is faith *and* good works, Scripture *and* tradition, grace *and* nature. The "and" operates in other ways also, "local church and universal church" being one example. The "and" also demands that national boundaries and ethnic differences not exclude people from the church.

The "and" is what Catholicism is about. Claiming to be Catholic means that we claim to be a church that is for all. It is not a matter of either/or but of both/and.

Eastern Europe

The elimination of religion was a high government priority in the countries that fell under Soviet influence after World War II. Religious practices were forbidden; churches, seminaries, convents and monasteries closed, Bibles confiscated. Women and men who were caught teaching or practicing their faith were severely punished, often imprisoned, and sometimes killed. As it did in the early centuries of its history, the church went underground.

Men were secretly trained and ordained for priesthood. Reports from some of these priests tell of their leading a double life that even some of their families were unaware of. By day they worked in the factory or office, and by night they served the embattled church. There have also been reports that at least three women were ordained in Czechoslovakia.

In 1992, the Vatican issued a statement that all acts performed by the underground priests were considered valid. Baptisms, Eucharists, marriages, and the Sacrament of the Sick were not questioned, but some of the secretly ordained priests were told that they were not allowed to continue in public ministry. Single men could apply for formal ordination, but married men could serve as deacon or apply for formal ordination in the Greek Catholic Church. Many priests obeyed, but some continue to serve the communities that they nourished during the communist regime.

However minimal their participation, the Catholic churches from every Eastern European country except atheist Albania had representatives at some sessions of Vatican II. Their presence, however, depended on receiving permission from government officials. In some countries a few bishops were permitted to travel while others were not, in an attempt by the government to create a split among them. One cardinal from Czechoslovakia was permitted to attend the last session of the council but not allowed to return to his country.

The effects of as well as participation in Vatican II varied from country to country. In Yugoslavia, for instance, a weekly bulletin announced news of the council. This facilitated liturgical changes there more easily than in any other Eastern Bloc country. Poland was able to spread the news through pastoral letters and "conciliar" sermons. Limited editions reached Czechoslovakia but Catholics in Lithuania, Latvia, and Belorussia were deprived of the documents by the Soviet government. The availability of Bibles was just as restricted in Eastern Europe. In Romania, only priests could sell Bibles, but they had to report the name of every person who bought one.

While the faith of many shrivelled and died, underground churches in communist countries spawned a small but powerful group of laity who defended the church often at great cost. Their fierce loyalty is sometimes put to the test today, with nostalgia for the religion of the past in tension with directions proposed by the post–Vatican II church.

We in the United States can hardly imagine the joy of monks as they gathered in the cathedral in Prague in 1989 where, for the first time in forty years, they were permitted to wear their religious habit and to celebrate the Eucharist publicly. Nor can we know the exhilaration of Catholics as one after the other, Eastern Bloc countries restored church buildings as places of worship after using them as storehouses or museums. Or the excitement as parishes were reestablished, seminaries opened their doors again, convents and monasteries were reclaimed, and religious education programs for children and adult study groups formed.

The churches in Eastern Europe, marked as they are by decades of oppression as well as national rivalries, have deep roots. Catholicism has not been destroyed by these events, but it is facing redefinition amid trying circumstances as nations rebuild themselves and in some cases rediscover ancient rivalries. Maintaining the tradition they fought so long and hard for sometimes conflicts with the values of Vatican II that challenges them to move into the future.

Loyalty to the church in Eastern Europe is not universal. Forty years of communist oppression of religion has left many in the church somewhat rootless. Many young people do not have childhood memories of first communions, or the delight of Christmas or Easter. They do not have the experience of celebrating significant moments in life as marriage or funerals in relation to God or to the church. It is no wonder that evangelization has become a dominant theme in Pope John Paul's speeches and writings.

By respecting, preserving, and fostering the particular values and riches of your people's cultural heritage, you will be in a better position to lead them to a better understanding of the mystery of Christ, which is to be lived in the noble, concrete, and daily experience of African life... It is a question of bringing Christ into the very center of African life, and lifting up all African life to Christ. Thus not only is Christianity relevant to Africa, but Christ in the members of his body is himself African.

–Pope John Paul II, *"The African Bishops Challenge,"* 1980

Africa

One of the destructive ideas that militated against Africans responding to the gospel was the idea (fostered by some missionaries) that Africans were the children of Ham, the accursed son of Noah. Ham was cursed by his father for not covering his (Noah's) nakedness when Noah was drunk. That curse made his descendants slaves to those of his brothers. Scholars suggest that the story may have been told to justify the slavery of one people by another. In any case, applying it to Africans (perhaps as a justification of slavery) left the people with a negative sense of themselves and of Christianity. This belief was so strong even at the end of the nineteenth century that missionary bishops at the First Vatican Council composed a prayer asking God to free the African continent from the curse of Ham.[3]

In spite of negative attitudes, such as the "children of Ham" epithet, the African continent has, in this century, been able to move from colonial status to that of independence. That move leaves some African nations facing problems of ethnic and tribal conflicts, poverty and hunger, massive movements of refugees, and, in some places, despotic governments and war. The church is part of that experience even as it moves from a dependent missionary-directed church to a more self-defined one. Native clergy and lay ministers are attempting to bring the gospel into conversation with the unique problems of African peoples.

As for Eastern European churches, so is evangelization also the major theme for the churches in Africa. The 1994 Synod on Africa insisted that simply translating church doctrine and practices into the vernacular has proven to be ineffective, and what is required is real and long-term attempts at incarnating Christian values into African society. The church evangelizes by preaching the word, celebrating the sacraments, witnessing by Christian lives, and ministering to those in need — all this in an attitude of profound respect for the people's experience of God in their lives. Evangelization cannot look as if Christianity is a foreign import.

The church in Africa does not have the same long tradition of Catholicism as the church in Eastern Europe. In spite of arriving on the continent very early and making significant contributions to the early church, Christianity did not take firm root in Africa.

Yet, the legacy left by the erudite and creative African St. Augustine, bishop of Hippo (in present day Algeria) has had a major influence on theology for more than fifteen hundred years. Augustine's teaching determined how centuries of Christians thought about God, what it means to be human, and what the church is. He defended the equality of the three persons of the Trinity at a time when others taught that the Son and the Spirit were subordinate to the Father. His description of the relationship among the persons of the Trinity as "Lover, Loved, and Love" stands today as a helpful way of thinking about our trinitarian God. On the other hand, his views of original sin accounted for the universal presence of evil among human beings, and his insis-

tence that everyone outside the church is lost gave a particular face to that evil.

There were some missionary efforts in Africa in the fifteenth and sixteenth centuries, but the advance of Islam wiped out many traces of it. In places where the church did survive, the practice of Catholicism is modeled on that of Europe or North America, the faith coming as it did with the colonizers. Music, art, customs, feasts, and celebrations all reflect a foreign influence. Distinguishing between what is essentially Catholic Christian and what is of a foreign culture results in efforts to de-Westernize the church in some areas. Evangelization in those places looks very different from that carried out now in areas where Christianity is taking root for the first time.

In the past three decades, the number of Catholics in Africa has more than doubled. In the 1950s, there were two native bishops; today there are hundreds, seminaries are full, and the number of baptisms increases year by year. In St. Joseph's Church in Benin City, Nigeria, in 1988, 368 adults were baptized, about two hundred of them by immersion. The church in Africa is vibrant and dynamic; it is not a clone of a

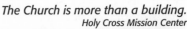

The Church is more than a building.
Holy Cross Mission Center

European church. The culture of the clan, associated as it is with religious sensibilities, determines how Christianity is accepted, lived, and celebrated.

The drama of African liturgy incorporating traditional dance, music, vestments, and community involvement sometimes startles Westerners. Such behaviors do not look like the Western brand of Christianity.

Liberty is celebration of culture, of life
Holy Cross Mission Center

And that is just the point. The outward celebrations and rituals, important as they are to the life of the community, are also signs of what is occurring in the faith experiences of the people. Becoming Christian does not mean learning to celebrate and worship in the ways of the West. Nor, does it mean opting for Western styles of living out the faith.

But becoming Christian also raises questions about strong and powerful African customs. Polygamy is one of the stabilizing forces in some African societies. It not only replaced a system of slavery, it is also the basis for the economy, providing workers from the family rather than from spoils of war. The security of the family economy is also insured by a practice similar to the Hebrew levirate law of the Old Testament. When a man dies, his brother is required to take the widow and her children.

Polygamy remains a hurdle for some who wish to be baptized. The question for some African theologians is whether traditional Christian forms of marriage are the only ones ap-

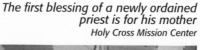
The first blessing of a newly ordained priest is for his mother
Holy Cross Mission Center

propriate for Christians. When a powerful chief wishes to be baptized, Canon Law would require him to give up all but one of his wives. The question then is what is to become of the wives who must be rejected if a husband is baptized? The social and economic upheaval pales in the face of the disgrace and rejection that the women would experience.

Many African bishops were born into and raised in polygamous families. In fact, a cardinal once told reporters in Rome that his father, a very important chief, had more than a hundred wives.

No one is making a case for perpetuating polygamy but for an understanding of the culture that had depended on polygamy as a stabilizing influence. The presumption (and the hope) is that as the role of women changes in polygamous societies and as women become more educated, the practice will lose its force. In the meantime, pastoral questions arise about Christianizing men and women whose whole life is involved in the practice. Perhaps some privilege similar to the Pauline or Petrine privilege could be developed for the "benefit of the faith."

The Pauline privilege states that a marriage between two persons who are not baptized may be set aside when one party converts to Catholicism and wishes to remarry. It is based on 1 Corinthians 7:12–16, in which Paul spells out the reasons why a convert may leave a nonbelieving partner.

The Petrine privilege developed as a result of situations in the United States. It allows the pope to dissolve a marriage between a Christian and a non-Christian. In either case, the marriage was not sacramental in the first place. Only marriages between two baptized Christians may be sacramental. Neither privilege is granted casually; there must be serious reasons.

Another issue is that of the celibacy of priests. More than two decades ago, 83 percent of the native priests in Zaire supported optional celibacy for priests. Family and children are so important that celibacy is not understood, nor is it accepted and respected as a value in many areas. Not to have children is a great disgrace. Celibate priests are suspect. In such a situation, the witness value of celibacy is deemed by some to be questionable. The symbolic question is aggravated by the number of Catholic communities that are not regularly able to celebrate the Eucharist because there is no celibate priest available.

African nations are as dissimilar from one another as are the countries of other continents. In speaking of the church in Africa, I do not mean to minimize those differences. While there are some common issues, it is important to remember the differences in history, geography, climate, and culture that distinguish one country from another.

Asia

When we turn our attention to Asia, the faces of the church become even more varied. The histories of the church in China, Japan, the Philippines, or other Asian countries require that we do not speak of the church in Asia as if they were greatly similar.

The Philippines[4] is the most Catholic country in Asia. To foster this Catholicity, Maryknoll Fa-

Ordaining native clergy.
Holy Cross Mission Center

thers, inspired by the basic Christian communities (BCCs) in Latin America, set up structures for the celebration of liturgies according to the norms of the Vatican Council. The focus of these groups soon turned to leadership training for the laity. In rural areas, lay persons led non-Eucharistic services, prepared couples for marriage, and conducted funerals in the absence of a priest. Catholic communities grew without benefit of the leadership of the clergy and therefore without regularly celebrating Eucharist.

Connections between faith and the political and economic realities of life led many BCCs to action on behalf of the poor and to concern for human rights. One military report claimed that "the Basic Christian Communities have become the most potent political force of the Church in the Philippines today."

The worldwide television coverage of the overthrow of the Marcos regime witnessed to the influence of the church and especially of the movement of BCCs. But Mary John Mananzan, O.S.B., dean of St. Scholastica's College in Manila, maintains that

The gifts of all enrich the liturgy.
Holy Cross Mission Center

because of the fear of communism, basic Christian communities are now slowly being reshaped into "basic *ecclesial* communities" that focus more of their energies on internal church affairs, thus lessening their impact on the society at large.

Mananzan also laments the turn toward fundamentalism among many Charismatic Catholics, the Cursillos, and the Focolare movement. On a more positive note, she writes of the growth of interest in Oriental forms of spirituality and of commitment to prayer and social justice on the part of many Filipino Catholics.

The story in China is very different from that in the Philippines. The church in China has been devastated by decades of oppression that resulted in two separate but related "churches," one the approved "official church" and the other the "underground church." One reason for this is that the Chinese church was caught in a web precipitated by events in Italy. To protect the Italian church, Pius XII prohibited cooperation with communist governments. When Chinese bishops obeyed the pope, the Chinese government retaliated with a demand that all churches observe three autonomies: self-government, self-support and self-propagation. The Chinese church could not obey any foreign ruler, accept foreign money, or depend on foreign missionaries. This effectively required a decision on the part of Catholics whether to remain in union with Rome or to comply with the government.

Some bishops, priests, and lay persons, in order to continue to practice their faith, renounced their allegiance to the pope. Others became an underground church, refusing to take that oath. In the face of the same crisis, different persons made different choices from different motivations. But as they are now able to speak to one another, there is, for the most part, a sense of acceptance of, if not respect for the motivation that inspired each choice.

While the Catholics who would not disassociate themselves from the pope were more severely punished, clergy and laity in both camps were imprisoned or exiled. The greatest desire of the state-recognized church, according to Father Joseph Zen Erjwun, a Hong Kong theologian, is to be reunited with the pope. He writes that it would be "cruelty to wish them to remain in this forced separation from where their heart is."[5]

One bishop from the official church tells a story about sending two priests to the village where Mao was born to begin to evangelize. When they arrived, they found a small community of Catholics who had kept the faith alive with only the rosary to cling to. They counted the prayers on stones or knots in a cord, but they repeated the prayers and taught them to the next generation. They knew the Creed, the Hail Mary, and the Lord's Prayer. The fifteen mysteries of the rosary helped them remember the life of Jesus.

While the ecclesial issues in China do involve the developments of Vatican II, the most crucial issue centers around the reconciliation of the two churches.

As different as the Philippines and China are from each other, Japan presents yet another Asian face of the church. Only 400,000 out of a population of 120,000,000 are Catholic. That translates to one out of every three hundred.

The bishops' conference of Japan has identified the fundamental problem in evangelizing the country as "the separation between faith and life and between the church and society." The Japanese people enjoy one of the greatest degrees of religious liberty of any nation in the world. Cults attract many who are searching for answers to the complex anxieties of their lives. That may be in part because their educational system has been criticized as including ideas that do not foster the development of the person.

The quest for spiritual values in Japan was reported in Tokyo's daily newspaper, *Asahi Shimbun*. When people were asked, "What do you give preference to, the satisfaction of your material needs or your spiritual needs?" 80 percent chose spiritual needs. The archbishop of Tokyo, Peter Shirayanagi, has spoken frequently of the spiritual hunger evident among the people. The church is searching for ways to answer that hunger without falling into the trap of the cults, providing quick and easy answers to profound questions.

Latin America

South America is the birthplace of liberation theology, that branch of theology that uses as its starting point the lives of the poor and oppressed. Unlike Asia and Africa, the Catholic church has been firmly entrenched on the continent for centuries and was ready for the call of the council. The Latin American episcopal conference (CELAM), having been established in 1955, was relatively strong, strong enough, in fact, to convene meetings during the sessions of the council. In spite of that, the 620 bishops who were present had little influence on the final documents. Liberation theology had not yet been developed. The Latin American church had not yet found its own voice.

Shortly after the council, the church moved from identifying itself as the church for the poor to using John XXIII's term, "the church of the poor." At first, attempts were made to renew the liturgy and the spirituality of the people according to Vatican guidelines, but the religion of the people

Archbishop Oscar Romero was martyred while saying Mass.
Notre Dame Magazine

was so strong that the official church had to respect the more indigenous expression of the faith rather than follow Roman guidelines.

The post–Vatican II church was caught in the web of military repression in Brazil, Bolivia, Uruguay, Chile, Peru, Argentina, El Salvador, and Nicaragua. Some in the church, laity and clergy alike, took a sharp swing to the right. Others identified even more strongly with the oppressed. The names of the martyrs Oscar Romero, Ita Ford, Dorothy Kazel, Maura Clarke, Jean Donovan, the six Jesuits, and two women workers are only a few representatives of the thousands who suffered and died.

The division in the church in Latin America is different from that in Eastern Europe or in China. It is primarily one between classes. After a first exuberant response to the council, developments have been more conservative. The work of liberation theologians has been restricted, supporters of liberation theology are not being appointed bishop,

The Diversity of the Church

Sent to all peoples of every time and place, the church is not bound exclusively and indissolubly to any race or nation, nor to any particular way of life or customary pattern of living, ancient or recent. Faithful to her own tradition and at the same time conscious of her universal mission, she can enter into communion with various cultural modes, to her own enrichment and theirs too.

Gaudium et Spes, #58

and the spirit of collegiality that gave CELAM its strength is being replaced by a group of autonomous bishops who are more closely related to Rome than to each other.

In spite of these drawbacks, tens of thousands of Christian base communities are flourishing, and liberation theology defines the faith-sharing that is done in these communities. Lay women and men are assuming leadership, especially in those areas where there are no priests. A sister missionary in northern Brazil told me that she does not speak to the people about being a sacramental church because they have the Eucharist only once a year. "All I have to give is the Word." This may be one of the reasons why so many in Latin America are flocking to evangelical churches.

Inculturation

This discussion of the differences in the practice of the Catholic faith is meant to provide a better understanding of just what it means to be Catholic. It is not that one brand of Catholicism is *the one* by which others are to be measured, but rather that each is one of many manifestations of church. Each of these faces of the church is church. Each brings gifts and treasures that may enrich the others.

In facing this great diversity and out of respect for the religious heritage of the people, the church has adopted a policy of inculturation. Inculturation is not adaptation. Though efforts at adaptation took the differences in culture seriously and made some adjustments regarding the customs and history of

a people, it has been criticized as a subtle form of imposition that only makes superficial and peripheral accommodations. In 1974, the African bishops declared adaptation completely out of date and called for incarnating the gospel into African life.

As trying to understand what is meant by inculturation, we might look to the example of the early church, which did not require Gentile converts to become Jews in order to follow Jesus. They did not impose circumcision on the non-Jewish converts but allowed the message of Jesus to speak to the lives of the people and be accepted by them. The customs and practices of the Gentiles may have been different; it was not necessary for them to deny all of their practices. What was necessary was belief in the life, death, and resurrection of Jesus, fidelity to his teachings, and the rejection of anything that might threaten that faith.

Inculturation, a deeper process than adaptation, refers to transforming a culture from within in the light of the gospel message. "From within" is the key to understanding what is meant here. Perhaps a story will help. In the sixteenth century, Matteo Ricci, S.J. went to China as a missionary. He had ideas that were at odds with the understanding of missionary activity of the time.

He took seven years to study the Chinese language and lifestyle. He dressed and wore his hair like a mandarin, he adopted their style of eating, living, and studying; he entered their life so well that he began to think like the Chinese. When he studied their religion, he saw some practices that

Call for Inculturation

What could be more absurd than to try to transplant France, Spain, Italy or some other part of Europe into China? It is not these that you have to introduce but the faith, which will never despise or violate the rites and usages of any people provided they are not perverse but instead intend to safeguard and strengthen them.

Propaganda Fides, 1659

from the perspective of outsiders appeared to be in conflict with Christianity but, seen from within the culture, were not.

Ricci's study of Chinese culture convinced him that the Chinese words *T'ien* (heaven) and *Shang-ti* (Sovereign Lord) did not refer to some material reality but the true God whom he himself preached. Others held that the use of these words could be misconstrued by the masses and lead to a superstitious understanding of God.

Another point of conflict had to do with traditional rituals in honor of ancestors. The Chinese rites that paid tribute to ancestors were, in the eyes of some, mere superstition, or worse, ancestor worship. Rituals in honor of Confucius were interpreted as adoring him. Ricci became convinced that the rites were not religious either as originally instituted or as practiced by educated people. He was able to see connections with the Christian doctrine of the Communion of Saints and to present that in such a way that the faith was neither diluted nor in conflict with some traditional Chinese values.

For more than one hundred years the conflict over the Chinese rites was waged by Jesuits, who, for the most part, supported Ricci's ideas and Dominicans, who saw the rites as a threat to the Christian faith. The Vatican issued statements at various times supporting one or the other side but eventually and finally came down against the rites in 1742.

Ricci was not the only one who found points of similarity between the religion of the people he served and Christianity. In India, Roberto de Nobili learned to live as a sannyasi, a holy man of the Hindu people. He studied the Hindu holy books, lived, dressed, ate and spoke in the manner of the sannyasi, respecting native customs and usages. In this way, the people could recognize him as a holy person and hear his message. He too was criticized but the Vatican upheld him. The national seminary in Puna, India carries his name.

Only in recent years are the insights of Matteo Ricci and Roberto de Nobili receiving the attention they deserve. As we are coming to appreciate the meaning and importance of inculturation, we are not so quick to condemn all practices of other religions that we do not fathom. On the other hand, we do not try to "baptize" every custom indiscriminately. Some religious beliefs are in concert with Christian faith and others are not.

The church that is taking root on all continents is enriched not only by the music, art, and ritual of non-Western cultures, but also by the contributions of the people who live their lives according to gospel values and by theologians who write from their people's experience and tradition. The impact that this fresh look at the gospel will have on more traditional forms of Christianity is still unknown.

In somewhat the same way, inculturation calls upon the Euro-American form of Christianity to allow the good news to speak to the lives of Western peoples. The response will be different, to be sure, but will grow out of the history and culture of the people. Christianity will transform the culture from within.

Inculturation seeks out those hints of God's abiding presence that are already present in a culture. It searches for points of intersection between cultures and Christianity. It takes the music, art, family customs, feasts, and values of the community seriously. There is no reason for a culture to be destroyed nor for a people to deny their history in order to become Christian. There is no reason for peoples to become Europeanized in order to become Christian.

Christianity is not a transplanted religion that cuts people off from their ancestors and their traditions. This is a lesson we have learned too late for the Native Americans but one that the pope has been emphasizing as the church experiences growth in Africa, Asia, and Latin America. Inculturation comes into play in Eastern European countries struggling to reclaim their Christianity after decades of communist control. In each case, Christianity will take on the color of the culture. Chinese vestments, African drums, Indian sitar music and dance all contribute to the celebration of the Eucharist.

But inculturation goes deeper than externals such as vestments, music, and dance. The church is concerned about the essence of Christianity that must be transmitted and about what may be open to alteration. The question is not an easy one. While the *Decree on Ecumenism* speaks of a hierarchy of truths, it does not list the truths that must be believed except faith in "God, one and three, in the incarnate Son of God, our Redeemer and Lord" (#12). Building on that firm foundation, the church seeks to transform societies in a way that reflects trinitarian and incarnational faith.

Notes

1. Richard McBrien, *Catholicism* (San Francisco: Harper & Row, 1994), 723–24.
2. Karl Rahner, *Concern for the Church: Theological Investigations XX*, 2d ed. (New York: Macmillan, 1988), 110.
3. Walbert Bühlmann, *The Coming of the Third Church* (Maryknoll, N.Y.: Orbis Books, 1976), 151.
4. See Gaspar and Cacyan, "BCC in a Rural Setting," *Witness* 1:4 (1981), 63, and Mary John Mananzan, O.S.B., in Adrian Hastings, ed., *Modern Catholicism* (New York: Oxford University Press, 1991) for a fuller discussion of the church in the Philippines..
5. Jwun Zen-Er, "Did Chinese Catholics Die for a Secondary Truth?" *Origins* 23:41 (March 25, 1993), 714ff.

8

Issues Facing
the Church of the Future

"The past is prologue." Telling stories about our forebears, fascinating as they may be in themselves, is a way of learning about how they handled their trials and triumphs and of gleaning insights from their wisdom. It is one way of becoming wise ourselves. We reflect on the past — ancient times and yesterday — in order that we may better live today. While it may have been interesting to discover anecdotes and trivia about the church in earlier times, the main point is to learn to live the gospel today.

Living the gospel today involves creating a new future, just as the decisions that were made in the past affect our lives. What we do as individuals and as a church affects future generations and makes it easier or more difficult for them to be Catholic Christians. We do not, of course, exist simply to prepare for the future, but we are responsible to posterity for the church we continue to create.

In this chapter, I will suggest some of the issues that I believe this generation is responsible for facing. Our issues are not those of the first or the nineteenth centuries; they are not those of the church on other continents; our solutions will not be theirs. The issues we face arise out of our unique experience as Catholics who are also Americans. While the title of the chapter implies the future, it is really about today, for the future and the present are intricately entwined.

Today's Issues

In writing about the church after Vatican II, Denis Doyle described the concerns of two different groups of Catholics.[1] At one end of the spectrum are groups like Chicago's Call to Action, a lay group that thinks that the church has not yet begun to live out the ideals of the Second Vatican Council. Among its concerns listed in a February 1990 ad in the *New York Times* are:

- the involvement of women in all levels of ministry and decision-making;
- allowing married priests;
- consultation with the laity on sexual matters;
- involvement of the laity and clergy in the selection of bishops;
- academic freedom and due process for theologians;

- concrete steps toward resolving differences with other Christians;
- movement away from an authoritarian style of leadership.

A few months later, the Catholic Theological Society of America issued a similar but more nuanced statement calling for similar changes.

On the other end of the spectrum are those who believe that the directives of Vatican II have been misinterpreted and that what is needed is a return to the discipline and structures of the past. The Fellowship of Catholic Scholars are representative of this group. Among their concerns listed in a 1990 statement entitled "Vatican II: Promise and Reality — the Catholic Church in the United States Twenty-Five Years After Vatican II" are:

- the decline in the number of Catholics who attend Mass weekly;
- ignorance of the teachings and discipline of the church, especially among the young;
- secular mindsets and relativism regarding religious affiliation;
- divorce and invalid marriages;
- decline of Catholic schools;
- decline in the number of priestly and religious vocations;
- Catholic colleges that do not promote orthodoxy among students.

Most Catholics are somewhere in the middle, agreeing with some of the concerns of both groups. In a study Doyle did with colleagues, a good deal of diversity was seen among both laity and professional theologians. Most parishoners tended to be more traditional than most theologians, who held more subtle middle positions. The tensions between the two extremes identify the controversial issues that still need to be addressed, but they do not necessarily divide the church. "Catholic," as we have already noted, means there is room for all. And that means that we have to learn to live with disagreement.

The questions that Catholics today and in the near future have to deal with concern both internal affairs and the relationship between the church and the world. Doyle identified internal issues that we might collect under the headings *ecumenism, evangelization, authority, ministry,* and *ordination.* Labelling the issues internal and external in no way implies a sacred/secular split. All space and time is sacred, filled as it is by God's presence.

Perhaps the two lists do not focus on so-called external issues because their concern was what was to be done so that the church may better carry out its mission to the world. The church exists not for itself but for the world, and so we must look at the problems of our world through the lens of Christianity and ask what the gospel demands of us. I will focus on two of these in external issues: ecological issues and social justice.

Theologians, both professional and amateur, are addressing each of the topics and the relationships that may exist among some of them. Having peered into the past and taken a long look at the present state of the church, we will now project into the future imagining some of the unfinished business that faces Catholics.

Internal Issues

Ecumenism

The division that exists among Christians strikes at the heart of Jesus' saying that "by this will everyone know that you are my disciples, if you have love for one another" (John 13:35). In this century great efforts have been made to heal the wounds that still remain because of centuries-old antipathies and hatred among Christians of different denominations.

Ecumenism is not a burning issue in most parishes. In fact, if you were to browse through the indexes of some newly published books on American Catholicism, you would not find ecumenism listed. Yet, the brokenness that exists in the Body of Christ has been called a great scandal. Critical work is being carried out by Catholic and Protestant theologians to repair that scandal, but it is not yet a major concern for most Catholics. This longed-for unity fits well with the American agenda, given the multicultural and pluralistic nature of our society.

In the aftermath of World War II, most major Protestant churches met in Holland in a show of Christian unity. They decried the responsibility Christians had in the destruction of so much of the earth and the killing of so many children, women, and men. Centuries of religious prejudice on all sides made them aware of the difficulties they faced, but they pledged themselves in forceful words: "Here at Amsterdam, we have committed ourselves afresh to Him and have convened with one another in constituting the World Council of Churches. We intend to stay together."

This was not the first such council; there had been earlier efforts, but two movements that laid the groundwork are especially notable: the Faith and Order Movement and the Life and Work Movement. Pius XI forbade Catholics to attend these conferences because their presence might seem to condone "false Christianity" and to constitute a denial that the only way to unity was a return to Rome.

While Catholics were not permitted to attend the Amsterdam meeting, some Catholic ecumenists were able to persuade Pius XII in 1950 to allow dialogues among Catholics and Protestants. Two years later, the Catholic Conference for Ecumenical Questions held its first meeting with the permission of the pope. In 1960 the Secretariat for the Promotion of Christian Unity held its first annual meeting.

The Roman Catholic Church still does not belong to the World Council of Churches, but a Joint Working Group of the WCC and the Catholic Church has been working on three significant issues: ecumenism, the way to achieve unity, and approaches to social issues. Catholics are also members of the Faith and Order Commission of the WCC and contributed to the important document *Baptism, Eucharist and Ministry.* When the WCC met in Australia in 1991 they agreed that the presence of the papacy was no longer a hindrance to unity; rather, it was the papacy's absence from the discussions that hindered ecumenism.

The language in ecumenical circles has developed along with theology. When John XXIII called the Second Vatican Council, his dream was of a united Christianity. In fact, some feared that his "ecumenical" council meant a meeting of Catholics, Protestants, and Orthodox Christians. John's words, while a break from the statements of earlier popes, are a clear indication of the fragile state of the question. He spoke of "separated brethren" and "fraternal reunion in the embrace of the ancient common mother."

The Decree on Ecumenism (*Unitatis Redintegratio*) may look somewhat tame at this point in history, and that may be a sign of just how much has been accomplished since its promulgation. The acknowledgment that "both sides were to blame" for the divisions in the church was a breakthrough of major proportions, as was the reference to other Christian denominations as "churches" and as ecclesial communities.

The images of Pope Paul VI and Patriarch Athenagoras embracing and of Pope Paul kissing the feet of Bishop Meliton, representative of the Holy

Worship and Christian Unity

As for common worship, however, it may not be regarded as a means to be used indiscriminately for the restoration of unity among Christians. Such worship depends chiefly on two principles: it should signify the unity of the Church; it should provide a sharing in the means of grace. The fact that it should signify unity generally rules out common worship. Yet the gaining of needed grace sometimes commends it.

Decree on Ecumenism, #8

Synod of Constantinople, symbolize the ecumenical attempts between the Orthodox Church and the Catholic Church. Voiding of the mutual excommunications imposed by each church on the other in 1054 made possible the on-going dialogue between the Eastern and Western churches.

The Graymoor Fathers (an American community based in New York) encouraged Catholics to pray for Christian unity during one week every January. The Octave for Christian Unity predated Vatican II, and the prayers were that Protestants would mend their ways and pledge allegiance to Rome. But after the council, we became more aware that, "there can be no ecumenism worthy of the name without a change of heart"(*Decree on Ecumenism*, #7). That difficult change of heart includes both individual and institutional conversion.

In the United States, the response to the council's call for ecumenical dialogue was spontaneous and energetic. In the years after the council, pastors exchanged pulpits, parishoners engaged in dialogues in parishes and in homes and shared common prayer services. The first flush of enthusiasm lasted only a few years, in part because not enough theological thought had been done in preparation for the process. After preliminary sharings, most Christians were not sufficiently informed about their own tradition to engage in meaningful dialogue.

The necessary groundwork is being undertaken by theologians such as those now engaged in Lutheran-Catholic and Anglican-Catholic bilat-

Interfaith Prayer Service
Catholic News Service

eral dialogues that focus on what is held in common as well as what separates us. No longer is the language of "separated brethren who need to return to Rome" the norm. Some of the most significant documents to come out of these conversations address critical topics such as Eucharist, ministry and ordination, justification by faith, and authority in the church.

One development witnesses to the advances that have been made. In the late 1960s and 1970s the question for many was whether Catholics and Protestants could pray together, and share non-Eucharistic celebrations. In the United States, that question has, for the most part, become a non-question. The issue today is about intercommunion, sharing the Eucharist.

The guidelines laid down by the Vatican regarding intercommunion apply only to persons whose faith in the Eucharist conforms to the Catholic Church's teaching. Besides the requirement that there must be a prolonged period without recourse to a minister of their own denomination, non-Catholics must experience a spiritual need and ask for the sacrament of their own accord. Of course, like Catholics, they must have the proper dispositions and lead worthy Christian lives.

The reunion of Christian churches does not depend on the workings of authority figures in the various denominations alone. Recent history teaches us that most changes begin on the grassroots level. Local efforts at mutuality and cooperative efforts may be more forthcoming in the

United States than in some other countries because of the multicultural nature of our society. Catholics no longer live in self-chosen ghettoes. Neighborhoods are more diverse. Catholics, Protestants, Jews, and Muslims are facing the same societal problems and are often cooperating in solving those problems. They know one another socially and in the workplace; they belong to some of the same clubs; they watch the same television and read the same newspapers; their children attend the same schools. Regardless of their religious affiliation, they are all affected by the American ethos.

Not too much should be made of the advances in this area. It would be a mistake to be overly optimistic about relationships among the various religious bodies. Racial and religious prejudices regularly flare up and remind us that merely issuing statements or studying the issue in scholarly fashion is not sufficient. What is called for is a change of heart, a conversion on the part of individual Christians and on the part of the church as a whole.

Evangelization

Evangelization has gotten a bad rap. Because of overzealous proselytizing or emotional, enthusiastic preaching on the part of TV evangelists, some think of evangelization as a thoughtless acceptance of a charismatic but anti-intellectual kind of Christianity. Moreover, the word has become identified with an ultraconservative and literalist interpretation of the Christian tradition.

The word *evangelization*, however, has strong roots. It refers to the gospel or good news of Jesus Christ and is being reclaimed by the church as a means of obeying the injunction, "Go therefore and make disciples of all nations" (Matt. 28:19.) To be Christian is to be called to evangelize. Ours is not a private kind of religion but one that requires that each of us proclaim the gospel, especially by the witness of our lives.

Evangelization is not about making new Catholics, adding to the number of churchgoers. It is about Christianizing our world, renewing it so that all may live in accord with the good news of Jesus.

Paul VI in his Apostolic Exhortation *Evangelii Nuntiandi* insists that the best means of evangelizing is by the witness of our lives. It is a case of the old adage that actions speak louder than words.

The Committee on Evangelization of the National Conference of Catholic Bishops in their 1993 statement "Go And Make Disciples" identify three facets of evangelizing Catholics. For those who are attempting to practice their faith, it is a call to ongoing growth and conversion; for Catholics who are so in name only, it is a call to re-evangelization; and for those who have altogether stopped practicing their faith, it is a call to reconciliation.

One of the strong impulses of the movement toward evangelization is the reconciliation of baptized Catholics who have, for whatever reason, distanced themselves from the church community. While the proportion of American Catholics is growing, Catholics are more likely than any other major religious group to leave the church. Variously called lapsed, fallen away, nominal, alienated or marginalized, they are nevertheless Catholic. We would do better to focus on the noun *Catholic* rather than on the negative adjectives.

A recent Gallup poll discovered about 15 million inactive Catholics in the United States, about eight hundred within the boundaries of an average parish. Their definition of inactive Catholic is someone who had not attended Mass at least twice in the past year, apart from weddings, funerals, Christmas, and Easter. We can get some idea of the extent of the problem by the criterion used. It leads us to wonder how high the number would be if inactive Catholics were considered to be those who had not attended at least six times a year, discounting weddings, funerals, Christmas and Easter; or if the criterion were only those who attend Mass every Sunday but have no other relationship with the church.

Many American dioceses and parishes are conducting programs to welcome home Catholics who, for one reason or another, had become alienated from the church. Among the best known are the Paulist Ministries for Reconciliation and the Re-

Membering Church Program. Whatever the name of the program, the aim is to heal the broken Body of Christ. That sometimes includes seeking forgiveness from the inactive Catholic who may have suffered unnecessarily from harsh judgments or misunderstandings.

Authority

It may be impossible for us to imagine a church such as that described by the First Vatican Council, so far have we come in redefining the relationship between the clergy and the laity. Indeed, the expression, "discipleship of equals," originated by theologian Elisabeth Schüssler Fiorenza, has moved quickly into popular usage. But the movement has not been without its problems, not the least of which is the questioning of authority.

Statistics indicating the erosion of authority within the Catholic Church abound. A New York Times/CBS poll found that among Catholics 18 to 39 years of age the following percentages are in favor of the specified issue:

—ordination of women, 68 percent
—optional celibacy for priests, 69 percent
—permitting divorce and remarriage, 80 percent

Vatican I:
A Different Model

But the Church of Christ is not a community of equals in which all the faithful have the same rights. It is a society of unequals, not only because some of the faithful are clerics and some are lay [persons], but particularly because there is in the church the power from God whereby to some it is given to sanctify, teach and govern and to others not.[2]

First Vatican Council, 1870

—the use of artificial birth control, 83 percent

The poll also indicates that 86 percent of that population think that good Catholics may disagree with the pope on issues such as birth control, abortion, and divorce.

This is not just an American phenomenon. In Catholic Ireland, 71 percent of persons between 18 and 35 reject the teaching on birth control; among Catholics in Canada the rate is 91 percent. In the Catholic Philippines, 69 percent favor the government providing free birth control for those who wish it.

The first public and widespread rejection of Vatican authority in modern times occurred when Pope Paul VI issued *Humanae Vitae* in 1968, reaffirming the ban on the use of artificial contraception. In an unprecedented show of dissent Catholic laity, theologians, and clergy publicly protested the pope's pronouncement. While the statement was not infallible, the assumption was that the faithful would receive it with the normally expected submission. But "dissent" had entered the Catholic vocabulary.

The decline of authority in the church is often marked from the issuance of *Humanae Vitae*. American Catholics, like Catholics around the world, rejected the teaching in great numbers; even some of the clergy spoke openly against it and were disciplined by their bishops. While it probably did not cause the change, it was the first sign that American Catholics, like many others, were depending on their own consciences rather than on the office of the hierarchy.

The American bishops issued "Human Life in Our Day" later the same year. In that pastoral letter, they acknowledged that it was possible to have "theological dissent from the magisterium. . . only if the reasons are serious and well-founded, if the manner of the dissent does not question or impugn the teaching authority of the Church and is such as not to give scandal."

Since that time, disagreement among American Catholics has been sufficient for the Vatican to call a special meeting of American archbishops in

1989. Some of the misunderstandings discussed were our pluralistic culture, the women's movement, and the effects of democracy on people's consciousness. While this has not eliminated the tension, it was hoped that it would provide a basis for further discussion.

The complexity of reasons why twentieth-century Americans have changed their attitudes toward authority staggers the mind. In the political realm, the Nuremberg trials after World War II revolted people who heard that individual men did not feel responsible for the Holocaust, or even for their part in it, because they were only doing what they were told. Other similar situations aggravated the issue: the destruction of Mei Lai when soldiers unthinkingly followed orders; the Watergate fiasco because some thought blind obedience a virtue.

Political events were not the only things that altered our perceptions of authority. American emphasis on independence and personal responsibility alters the role of authority figures. Our very system of government is designed to share authority and balance responsibility among individuals and groups.

Higher levels of education have produced more critically thinking Catholics. No longer do we assume that the priest is the best educated or even among the best educated in the parish. We have already discussed the increase in theological education among the laity. The resulting self-assurance as well as the Vatican II's encouragement of the laity to assume responsibility for the mission of the church have given rise to a more independent Catholic.

Persons in authority stand under much greater scrutiny than in the past. Personal gifts of leadership, more collaborative styles of governance, partnership in ministry, redefining power, and empowerment are only a few of the conversations taking place in parishes and dioceses. The delicate balance between the church's teaching on the primacy of conscience and the obedience owed to pastors and bishops is still in the process of being negotiated.

The issue of obedience to authority raises the question of the primacy of conscience. There are principles to be considered in making an argument for the inviolability of conscience. First, the teaching of the church must be respected and considered a major resource for moral decision-making. But if after reflection, study, prayer and consultation there is disagreement, persons who disagree must obey their consciences. Secondly, the values upheld by the church are not to be repudiated if there is disagreement in a particular concrete case. Thirdly, attention needs to be paid to other resources besides official teachings: Scripture, respected friends and relatives, scientific findings, and elements in culture that bear on the issue. These are not, of course, the final word, but they do contribute to the process of moral decision-making.

New Definitions of Ministry

For the first time in centuries, lay persons are accepting the responsibility for much of the ministry in parishes. About 20,000 lay women and men serve

In the Absence of a Priest

If the diocesan bishop should decide that due to a dearth of priests a participation in the exercise of the pastoral care of a parish is to be entrusted to a deacon or to some other person who is not a priest, or to a community of persons, he is to appoint some priest endowed with the power and faculties of a pastor, to supervise the pastoral care.

Canon 517.2

as professional ministers for at least half-time. The American bishops have referred to this group of professional lay ministers as "ecclesial ministers."[3] (*Ecclesial* refers to the church as mystery, as Body of Christ, while *ecclesiastical* refers to the church as institution.)

Perhaps at no time in history have great numbers of the laity been so well educated theologically. Each year, thousands of the laity study in colleges and universities, and attend workshops and lectures to prepare themselves better for ministry. At the same time, attendance at Sunday Mass has dropped about 35 percent since 1965. The corps of involved laity is increasing, but it seems that something else is operating in the rest of the community.

Ruth Wallace[4], who interviewed women serving as pastoral administrators, found that five of the twenty she interviewed were not listed in the diocesan directory as administrator. Lay administrators are able to perform many of the ministries that priests formerly did, except, of course, presiding at Eucharist and the sacrament of Reconciliation. The American bishops have issued guidelines for Sunday worship in the absence of a priest. Catholic communities here and around the world are gathering for worship but are not celebrating Eucharist regularly.

When college students were asked what priestly ministries could be performed by the laity, they answered: visiting the sick, marriage preparation, baptismal preparation, youth programs, adult discussion groups and marriage counseling. They thought that only lay people should be responsible for maintaining the financial books, buildings, and grounds. They would reserve to the priest presiding at Eucharist and Reconciliation. They also listed officiating at marriages and baptisms and preaching at Mass as reserved to the priest, which is an interesting phenomenon considering that deacons are able to do all three.

Guidelines provided by the hierarchy for pastoral administrators indicate just how ambiguous the situation is. Laity who are leading the community in non-Eucharistic services are not to approach the altar except at the time of communion. The lay ministers may wear an alb (the long white robe) but are not to wear a chasuble (the outer garment worn by the priest during Mass) or stole. Many women pastoral administrators are against using any clerical vestments because they feel it distances them from the congregation. In a parish that I sometimes visit, everyone has a stole that is worn on major feasts and anniversaries. Each is decorated with the symbols and dates of the sacraments received.

The secondary role played by the lay pastoral administrator is symbolized every Sunday. The rule is that only an ordained priest may preach immediately after the Gospel during the liturgy of the Word. Keeping the letter of the law means that the pastoral administrator may not give a homily but may give "reflections" at another point in the Mass. In some cases, the priest says a few words after the Gospel and the lay minister then preaches. In others, the priest gives a homily and the minister shares reflections later.

The visiting priest who is committed to ministry in another parish or in the chancery is sometimes put into an untenable situation. He does not know the community, and is not part of their lives, nor are they part of his life. One priest described it as not giving his heart to them, since he had already given it to his own parish. He is not really their pastor.

But the discomfort is not restricted to the lay pastoral administrator or the visiting priest. Parishoners who lose an ordained pastor are often angry and feel somewhat second-class. This may be exacerbated by the fact that most of these parishes are rural, small, and poor.

Research needs to be done now on alternative staffing for parishes. Future projections suggest that more and more parishes will be administered by lay persons, and that even when ordination patterns change, lay persons will be central to parochial life. Situational responses are inadequate; what is needed is a strong theological foundation for the practice of lay-led parishes. If the practice is contrary to the theological definition of the church, then it is doomed and ought never to have been initiated. If, however, it has theological grounding, it needs to be celebrated by the whole church and not interpreted as a temporary solution to a crisis situation. The sacramental nature of the Catholic Church is in jeopardy when so many local communities are unable to celebrate Eucharist regularly. That is perhaps the theological question of primary importance.

Critical as the involvement of the laity in ministry is, the question becomes more complex when that lay person is a woman. Most of the pastoral administrators are women, but that is not the only place where professional women ministers serve. They are found in hospitals, clinics, shelters for the homeless and battered women, and campus ministries. The 1983 revision of Canon Law opened the door for women to serve on the diocesan level as diocesan chancellors, auditors, assessors, defenders of the marriage bond, promoters of justice, and judges on diocesan courts. They may also be members of diocesan synods and financial and pastoral councils. But the "stained-glass ceiling" still appears to exist in the church; women are included, but in token numbers.

The conflict over the ordination of women is becoming more acute as younger generations who only know the post–Vatican II church and a post–Women's Movement society begin to question the validity of arguments against women's ordination. They grew up hearing the expression *woman priest* and seeing women minister in a wide variety of ways. Their reasoning about the issue is different from an older generation's.

Of the 19,000 parishes in the United States, about 11 percent have no resident priest. The 1990 Official Catholic Directory lists 210 parishes as administered by persons who are not ordained priests: 129 of them are administered by sisters, 47 by deacons, 19 by lay persons (other than sisters or brothers), 12 by brothers, and 3 by pastoral teams. These statistics are believed to be on the low side because some bishops are loathe to admit that lay persons are running parishes; they therefore list the priest who is the sacramental minister. As critical as the situation in this country is, we are not yet as bad off as other countries. In France more than 22,000 parishes are without resident priests. In Africa, every year there are two hundred fewer priests and two million more Catholics. Worldwide, 34 percent of Catholic parishes are without a priest.

The solution of importing foreign priests to American parishes has been criticized because cultural differences may interfere with the relationship between pastor and parishioners. It also goes against the practice of the church in other places, where native priests and bishops are preferred to missionaries from foreign countries. What is dreaded most, of course, is that parishes be closed.

Gerard Broccolo, past Director of the Ministerial Formation Department in the archdiocese of Chicago, suggests that there are four possible solutions to the priest shortage that would protect the central position of the Eucharist in the Catholic Church.[5] From the least radical to the most radical they are:

1. Ordain women and persons who are not celibate. This is not a change in doctrine only in discipline.

2. Delegate deacons (both permanent and those who will be ordained to the priesthood) to preside at Eucharist. This option is more radical but follows a precedent. In the early church, only bishops presided at Eucharist; when the number of Christians increased, they delegated priests to celebrate among distant communities.

3. Delegate lay leaders who do not hold ecclesial office to preside. This is an even more radical option, but it has a precedent in bishops delegating others in their place.

4. The most radical change is for the church to do nothing. Communities would either be left without the Eucharist or would take matters into their

own hands and delegate their own leader for the Eucharist. Broccolo sees this "rampant Congregationalism" as the most difficult to reconcile with the Catholic tradition.

External Issues

Ecology

Theology that is developed in each age depends on the wisdom and knowledge of that age. The theology of Thomas Aquinas, for instance, makes eminent sense in the light of the learning of his day. Some of his conclusions, however, do not hold up in the light of later developments in human experience.

God's Earth and Ours

Scientists calculate that the cosmos may have existed more than four-and-a-half billion years without human life. It is therefore a bit presumptuous for us to claim that all the wonders of the earth — the trees and bushes, the plants and flowers, the fish and birds and animals — were created for the benefit of human beings. Our relationship with the earth may have taken a different turn had we not interpreted the creation story as giving humanity "dominion" over the rest of nature.

Our misreading of the creation story supported an attitude that set us above the rest of creation as if all of it were created only for us and not for itself. But a careful reading of the second account of creation in Genesis makes us aware of the close connection between the earth and the creature whom God made from that earth. The play on the words *h'adam* (the creature) and *ha'a dama* (the earth) is sometimes forgotten, but when it is taken seriously, the story of creation connects the earth, the creature made from the earth, and the breath of God so closely that it is impossible to think of the creature being master or having dominion over the earth.

Instead of using the resources of the earth thoughtlessly, we are now being called to respectful and responsible relationship with the rest of God's creation. It is not simply a political issue but a theological one, since one of the important roles of theology is to address the significant issues of an era in the light of faith. Theologians therefore are probing the abundant treasure of Christian tradition for insights to help us to be more aware of the connection between our faith in God and our care of the earth.

Our awareness of the destruction of so many ecological systems, the extinction of 10,000 species each year, deforestation, toxic waste, the pollution of air and waterways, to say nothing of the threat of nuclear destruction, has caused us to look differently at our relationship with the earth and indeed with the cosmos. Passionist priest Thomas

Berry maintains that the destruction of the earth is as much of a loss to the human soul as it is to the earth. "We need the experience of the natural world to activate our emotions and our sense of the sublime. If we do not have this experience, or these wonderful natural phenomenon are destroyed or disfigured, then our experience of the divine is disfigured."[6]

We need to ask ourselves what responsibility we as Americans and as Catholics have in the face of this disaster. Statistics warn us that although we are only about 6% of the world's population, we use or abuse over half of the world's resources. How do we, the richest free nation ever to exist, use those riches for the good of the whole world?

One response could be guilt: guilt for having more than others, guilt for all the gifts, all the advantages, all the benefits of being American. But guilt, psychologists tell us, is not the best motivation for conversion. To feel guilty about being born in or coming to this country is futile. I am not suggesting that we excuse ourselves from a more responsible care for the plants, trees, animals fish and birds who share this planet with us, but maintaining that guilt is not energizing and will not bring about the necessary transformation.

The Need for Social Justice

In a hypothetical world village of 1000 persons:

there are 329 Christians, 174 Muslims, 61 Buddhists, 52 Animists, 3 Jews, 34 other (Sikh, Jains, Zoroastians and Baha'is, for instance),
216 claim no religion.
564 are Asian, 210 European, 86 African, 80 South American, 60 North American.
60 persons have half the income;
500 are hungry;
600 live in shanty towns;
and 700 are illiterate.[7]

World Development Forum

The Church and Justice

While the Church is bound to give witness to justice, she recognizes that anyone who ventures to speak to people about justice must first be just in their eyes. Hence we must undertake an examination of the modes of acting and of the possessions and lifestyle found within the Church herself.

Justice in the World (par. 40)

Another response could be acknowledgment of past errors and the assumption of a responsible stance toward the rest of creation. This is not just a civic duty or a social responsibility. The destruction of the earth is in direct violation of the faith that we profess. When God created the sky and the sea, the fishes and the animals, God saw that it was good.

As Americans, we have the resources, the personnel, and the intelligence to begin to heal the wounded earth. We need what sociologist Augusta Neal, a Sister of Notre Dame de Namur, calls a "theology of relinquishment," a theology that holds us more accountable because we have been more abundantly blessed.

Social Justice
We have discussed the central role the church has to play in the efforts to create a just and peaceable society throughout this work. But it would be remiss not to raise the issue when thinking about our responsibility to the future. The American bishops have insisted that action on behalf of justice is *constitutive* of the gospel. There is no way to claim to be a good Catholic Christian without a concern for and com-

mitment to the coming of the Reign of God, and that Reign involves the establishment of justice. We who are so blessed bear great responsibility for this.

It is not necessary to rehash the problems and crises that beleaguer people around the world. It may be better for us to focus our attention on a few principles of Catholic social doctrine. The first is the principle of subsidiarity that maintains that nothing is to be done by a higher body that can be done by a lower. (The language should not suggest a hierarchical division that values higher over lower.) This principle was originally invoked to protect unions and other voluntary societies from interference by governments. It has also been applied within the structure of the church itself.

The state or a "higher" ecclesiastical body is responsible only when "lower" bodies fail to carry out their responsibility. Another way of saying this is that citizens ought not leave to distant governments what needs to be taken care of locally, and that the faithful ought not leave to the hierarchy what is their responsibility.

The second principle, socialization, balances the first. We do not exist in a vacuum; what one group does or does not do affects the life of others. As the network of relationships among persons, cities, and nations becomes more complex because of modern technology, the state or "higher body" is required to intervene. We can see this principle operating within the church, for instance, when national conferences of bishops meet to discuss issues that cross diocesan lines.

It is important to maintain a healthy tension between the principles of subsidiarity and socialization. A third principle that also needs to main-tain a healthy tension between opposites might be called the principle of rights and duties. Every right carries with it a concomitant responsibility. Each person has the right to protection of basic human rights but at the same time the responsibility to guarantee those rights to others. This principle, too, applies within the church as it does in the rest of society.

Conclusion

There is a saying among theologians that theology is to faith as music theory is to music. We do not study music theory for its own sake. We study it in order to better appreciate music, to be able to hear the nuances and shadings that an untrained ear might miss. Music theory enhances and enriches the experience of both the musician and the listener.

So it is with theology. Interesting as it is in itself, we do not study theology for its own sake. Theology exists for the benefit of faith. Theology enables us better to know and appreciate our faith — but more importantly, it enables us to better live our faith.

That is the bottom line. It is not enough to critically reflect on faith. We must live according to what we have reflected on.

The branch of theology known as ecclesiology is the field of study concerned with gathering information about the church, but it does so to help us live our faith in a more intelligent and committed way as a Christian community. Christians reflect on what it means to be church so as to be able to carry out the two great commandments of Jesus — to love God with all our hearts and minds and souls, and to love our neighbor as ourselves.

Notes

1. Denis M. Doyle, *The Church Emerging From Vatican II: A Popular Approach to Contemporary Catholicism* (Mystic, Conn.: Twenty-Third Publications, 1993), 2–7.
2. Quoted by Avery Dulles in *Models of the Church* (New York: Doubleday, 1974), 43.
3. "Called and Gifted: The American Catholic Laity" (Washington D.C.: United States Catholic Conference, 1980).
4. Ruth Wallace, *They Call Her Pastor* (Albany: State University of New York, 1992). This section on women pastoral associates owes much to her research.
5. Gerard Broccolo, "Can We Have Prayer Without Father?" *Journal of Catholic Campus Ministry Association* (Spring 1986), 23.
6. Thomas Berry quoted by David Gonzalez, "Religion Putting Faith in Environmentalism," *New York Times*, November 6, 1994, 13.
7. Cited in Multifaith Resources, 45 Windy Hill Court, P.O. Box 128, Wofford Heights CA 93285–0128.

The Crossroad Adult Christian Formation Program

Crossroad's "How To" adult Christian formation books have stood the test of time. Successfully used in parishes and colleges since the mid–80s, they now come with Facilitator and Participant Guides, ready to meet the new needs of the 90s.

What makes the program special? The Crossroad Program:

- is specifically geared to the adult learner;
- provides a comprehensive, systematic approach to learning;
- adapts to individual, parish and other group needs;
- relates learning to everyday living;
- provides basic texts richly illustrated with photos, charts, and special materials designed for maximum pedagogical effect;
- provides study guides to help teachers and students understand and connect the content of each text with their own live experiences and the community in which they live;
- has been designed by faculty from the prestigious Loyola Institute for Ministry, New Orleans: Marcel J. Dumestre, Barbara Fleischer, and Reynolds Ekstrom;
- and is the most affordable program of its kind.

For information and suggestions on how learning groups across the U.S. are successfully using "The Crossroad Program," call Reynolds Ekstrom, Educational Sales Consultant, at (504) 364-1440, or write us at The Crossroad Publishing Company, 370 Lexington Avenue, New York, NY 10017.

1. The Crossroad Scripture Study Program

How to Read the Old Testament
0-8245-0540-9 $12.95 pb
Illus. 124 pp
Facilitator Guide
0-8245-7003-0 $5.95 pb
80 pp
Participant Guide
0-8245-7002-2 $4.95 pb
80 pp

How to Read the New Testament
0-8245-0541-7 $12.95 pb
Illus. 128 pp
Facilitator Guide
0-8245-7001-4 $5.95 pb
80 pp
Participant Guide
0-8245-7006-6 $4.95 pb
80 pp

How to Read the Apocalypse
0-8245-1280-4 $15.95 pb
Illus. 160 pp

2. The Crossroad Theology and Church History Study Program

How to Read Church History
Volume 1: From the Beginnings to the Fifteenth Century
0-8245-0722-3 $14.95 pb
Illus. 195 pp

Facilitator Guide
0-8245-7005-7 $5.95 pb
80 pp
Participant Guide
0-8245-7004-9 $4.95 pb
80 pp

How to Read Church History
Volume 2: From the Reformation to the Present
0-8245-0908-0 $14.95 pb
Illus. 209 pp
Facilitator Guide
0-8245-7007-3 $5.95 pb
80 pp
Participant Guide
0-8245-7006-5 $4.95 pb
80 pp
How to Understand the Creed
0-8245-0868-8 $14.95 pb
Illus. 164 pp
Facilitator Guide
0-8245-7008-1 $14.95 pb
80 pp
Participant Guide
0-8245-7009-x $5.95 pb
80 pp

3. The Crossroad Christian Living Study Program

How to Understand the Liturgy
0-8245-0867-X $11.95 pb
Illus. 164 pp
Facilitator Guide
0-8245-7010-3 $14.95 pb
80 pp
Participant Guide
0-8245-7011-1 $5.95 pb

How to Understand the Sacraments
0-8245-1026-7 $14.95 pb
Illus. 208 pp
Facilitator Guide
0-8245-7012-x $14.95 pb
80 pp
Participant Guide
0-8245-7013-8 $5.95 pb
80 pp

How to Understand Marriage
0-8245-0810-6 $14.95 pb
Illus. 96 pp

4. Crossroad Special Interest Courses

How to Understand Islam
0-8245-0981-1 $14.95 pb
Illus. 164 pp

How to Read the World
0-8245-0721-5 $10.95 pb
Illus. 126 pp

How to Understand God
0-8245-1047-X $12.95 pb
Illus. 144 pp

How to Read the Church Fathers
0-8245-1204-9 $19.95 pb
Illus. 184 pp